STYLE BIBLE

We hope you have lots of fun joining in the Stardoll world.
Remember to be safe online and never give out your Stardoll password,
email addresses, or any other personal information, including photos.

STARDOLL: STYLE BIBLE
A BANTAM BOOK 978 0 857 51101 0

First published in Great Britain by Bantam,
an imprint of Random House Children's Publishers UK
A Random House Group Company.

This edition published 2013

1 3 5 7 9 10 8 6 4 2

Stardoll.com is an ever-evolving website. This book was released in August 2013; however,
please be aware that updates and changes may have happened on Stardoll.com since then.

Exclusive Stardoll virtual gift can be found by locating the code and instructions within the pages
of this book. Gift codes can be redeemed until the expiry date 31.12.2014

Photos © Shutterstock Images LLC
Photo credits: Startraks Photo/Rex Features p236bl. VILLARD/SIPA/Rex Features p237tl.
Jim Smeal/BEI/Rex Features p237br. Startraks Photo/Rex Features p238bl. Startraks Photo/Rex Features p241br.

The Random House Group Limited supports the Forest Stewardship Council® (FSC®),
the leading international forest-certification organisation. Our books carrying the FSC label are
printed on FSC® certified paper. FSC is the only forest-certification scheme supported by the
leading environmental organisations, including Greenpeace. Our paper procurement policy
can be found at www.randomhouse.co.uk/environment

MIX
Paper from
responsible sources
FSC® C020056

Bantam Books are published by Random House Children's Publishers UK,
61–63 Uxbridge Road, London W5 5SA

www.**randomhousechildrens**.co.uk   www.**totallyrandombooks**.co.uk   www.**randomhouse**.co.uk

Addresses for companies within The Random House Group Limited can be found at:
www.randomhouse.co.uk/offices.htm

THE RANDOM HOUSE GROUP Limited Reg. No. 954009

A CIP catalogue record for this book is available from the British Library.

Printed in China

BANTAM
BOOKS

Hi, Stardolls, it's Ami here!

Welcome to the Stardoll Style Bible!

We've crammed every single page with fashion, fun and friendship. You can read about the hottest trends, get style tips for your MeDoll and learn how to live life like an A-lister!

There are heaps of natural spa recipes that you can make at home, plus tips on how to style your hair like a true Stardoll. Oh, and if you're dreaming of worldwide stardom, don't miss our essential guide to being famous!
You're going to love it all, guaranteed!

So, are you ready to style it up?
Come on, let's go!

Ami x

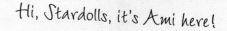

CONTENTS

STYLE SECRETS

Pssssst!
Honey, when it comes to fashion, you write the rules! The way you work your look is all down to you – just dress how you feel and express your awesome personality. Shine like a star!

Pssssst!
Whether you're creating a look for yourself or for your MeDoll, the secret is to start with just one item. It could be a printed scarf, a sequined dress, a jacket – anything! Once you've chosen your key piece, then you can build the rest of your outfit around it. Easy!

Pssssst!
Never underestimate the power of shoes! A gorgeous pair of strappy sandals or a pair of platform boots can give the same outfit a whole new vibe.

Psssst!
Prints, patterns and statement pieces are a big part of your style ID. But plain or neutral items like jumpers, tops, skirts and jeans can say just as much about you. Why don't you design something in the Stardoll Design studio to perfectly suit you?

Psssst!
There's no such thing as too many accessories, people! If you build up your collection, you'll always be able to style up your outfits in a flash!

15

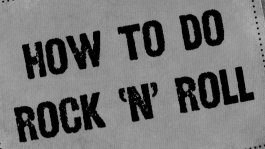

HOW TO DO ROCK 'N' ROLL

If you want to work the rock 'n' roll look, you've gotta have heaps of confidence and individuality. Rock chicks aren't afraid to express who they are, so let it loose, honey! Work the trend with band t-shirts, checked shirts, leggings, jeans and miniskirts. And hunt out classic rock patterns, like skull prints, spots and stars. This style is all about attitude!

STARDOLL DICTIONARY

Rock 'n' roll: *A classically rebellious style of music that's known for its edgy trends.*

Leather jackets are pure rock 'n' roll.

This studded bag is more rock 'n' roll than a drum kit!

Ripped tights and platforms scream 'I'm-with-the-band!'.

Turn over the page for more rock-tastic stuff!

Black is a great starting point for your rock 'n' roll palette, but don't steer away from colour. You can put a rocky spin on any shade you like, from electric blue to bubblegum pink. The secret is not to use too many colours in the same outfit. Just mix one or two main shades with black and you'll get the look bang on. Look out for industrial fabrics, tartan and shimmery sequins. And when you're choosing accessories, think rock star sunglasses, silver studs and gem-encrusted jewellery! Get styling, rock chick!

Use strong colours to create a totally rocky vibe.

Go for retro prints and band t-shirts.

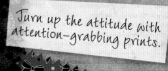

Turn up the attitude with attention-grabbing prints.

MEDOLL STYLE

Go for loads of black with bursts of bright colour. Then crank it up a notch with some totally rock-tastic accessories. Wristbands, pendants, studded belts . . . what will you choose for your MeDoll?

HOW TO DO COLOUR BLOCKING

Forget patterns, prints and embellishments – colour blocking is all about pure, plain colour. All tops, skirts, trousers, dresses, jackets and accessories should be totally unadorned. That's right, people – this look's about colour, colour, colour! Push the boundaries and add your own unique twist to the trend. How bright will you go?

STARDOLL DICTIONARY

Colour blocking: *1. Mixing two or more colours within an outfit. 2. Pushing the boundaries with brights, neutrals, bolds and pastels.*

Look out for the latest colour block tops.

Matchy-matchy shorts and trainers? We likey!

Go for stand-out accessories in plain 'n' pretty colours.

Turn over the page for more colour blocking ideas!

When it comes to choosing your colour blocking palette, it's all down to the way you feel. For a fresh, subtle look, start with a pale base, mix in a neutral shade, then add a zap of bright colour. Or go for fashion fireworks, with fizzy shades of orange, red, pink and blue. Pick out all the plain pieces in your wardrobe and try them on in different combinations. Use black, white, brights and neutrals to take this look in any direction you want!

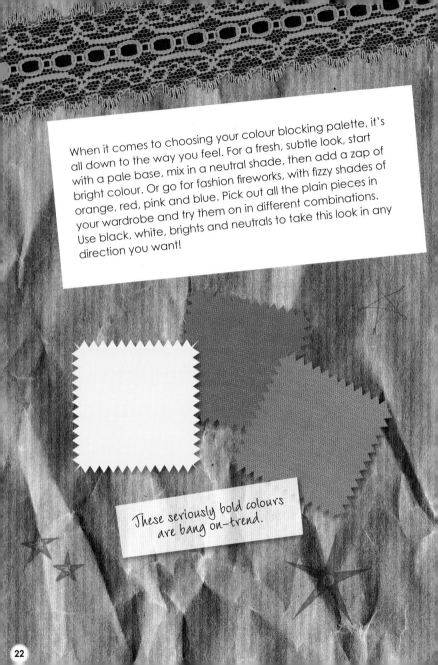

These seriously bold colours are bang on-trend.

Jewel-bright shades are magical and mysterious.

These pretty cupcake colours look good enough to eat!

MEDOLL STYLE

Short of Stardollars? No worries! You can start working this trend with your existing online wardrobe. Kick things off by accessorising a coloured dress with a bright belt and bag.

HOW TO DO CHIC

The chic trend is all about personal style choices. Look out for elegant designs and quality fabrics. Only the best will do! When it comes to hemlines, minis and maxis are off the menu – chic skirts and dresses are neat and knee-length. Trousers are tailored and jeans are never ripped or distressed. Put your own spin on this classic trend . . .

STARDOLL DICTIONARY

Chic: *A classically stylish way of dressing yourself or decorating your Suite. This look is understated and elegant.*

This gold dress puts a glamorous twist on the trend.

The knee-length hemline is oh-so-chic!

Check out the matching belt and shoes!

Turn over the page for more chic colours!

Being effortlessly chic is all down to your expert planning. This is a look that you just can't rush! Every item of your outfit must be carefully chosen. Do the textures of your fabrics work together? Are your colours and patterns elegant and stylish? Could you co-ordinate your shoes, belt and even your bag? Pick out the chicest items in your wardrobe, think through the details, then put together an outfit that's worthy of a Parisian catwalk!

It's official . . . chic colours never go out of style!

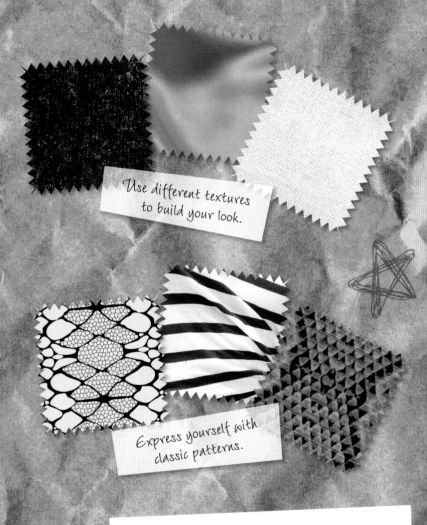

Use different textures to build your look.

Express yourself with classic patterns.

MEDOLL STYLE

Hit the Fashion Design studio and create a beautifully co-ordinated outfit. Keep things classic and simple, even when you're choosing your jewellery and accessories.

HOW TO DO PRIM AND PROPER

The prim and proper trend is fashion on its best behaviour! We're talking luxurious fabrics, smart tailoring and clean lines, with nothing cluttered or fancy in sight. It's all about simplicity and elegance, Stardolls! Get the look with billowing silk blouses, buttoned-up shirts, tailored trousers and super-smart skirts. Think grown-up, ladylike chic!

STARDOLL DICTIONARY

Prim: *Neat, tidy and totally formal.*
Proper: *Well-behaved, well-mannered, calm and controlled.*

A blouse and bow combo is the height of buttoned-up chic.

Check out the trousers! That's sharp tailoring, people.

Shoes with socks? Prim-o-rama!

Turn over the page for more prim and proper palettes!

29

The prim and proper trend demands a well-mannered colour palette. Most of your outfit should be plain and if you want to use prints, keep 'em subtle. Neutral shades like white, grey and fawn are spot on, and strong colours such as navy, burgundy and forest-green are perfectly prim and proper, too! If you want to do prints, keep the volume down low with tiny polka dots, geometric shapes and other low-key patterns. Loud and lively is out – this look is all about expressing your calm side!

Grey, cream, camel —
nail the trend with pales.

Keep darker colours calm and controlled.

Think subtle with your patterns and prints.

MEDOLL STYLE

Start with a tailored item, then build the look from there. Just one statement accessory is enough for this trend, so take your time finding something perfectly prim!

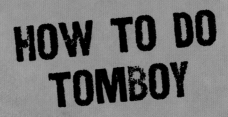

HOW TO DO TOMBOY

Don't panic, fashionistas! You don't have to get a Justin Bieber-style haircut or dress like JLS to work this look! The tomboy trend is about borrowing the coolest boy styles and making them a look that's all your own. Search for boy-cut jeans, oversized tees, polo shirts and boyfriend cardigans. You can take this trend any which way.

STARDOLL DICTIONARY

Tomboy: *A girl who puts her own cute spin on traditional boy colours and clothes.*

Slogan tees are totally tomboy. Make a statement!

Three-quarter length sleeves put a softer spin on boyish.

These tomboy feet look oh-so-sweet in brogues.

Turn the page for more colour tips from the lads!

33

The tomboy colour palette is all about the classic boy shades. You know, blue, black, white, brown, etc. Sure, you can do brights and pastels if you want, but be sure to mix them with those traditional boy colours. Tough fabrics like denim and corduroy are perfect for this look and so are the softer sportswear fabrics. Pick out the most boyish pieces in your wardrobe, borrow some accessories from your bro or best boy pal, and away you go!

Go totally tomboy in traditional boy colours.

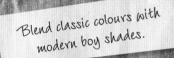

Blend classic colours with modern boy shades.

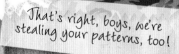

That's right, boys, we're stealing your patterns, too!

MEDOLL STYLE

You're bound to have something that fits this look.
Basic t-shirts, checked shirts, trousers and jeans . . .
Check out what you've got, then top up on tomboy
trends at the StarPlaza!

HOW TO DO GLAM ROCK

Glam rock style was inspired by the seventies music scene. If you've ever seen pictures of David Bowie singing in his spacesuit costume, you'll know all about it! The look is kinda theatrical, kinda spacey and majorly, majorly shiny and OTT! It sounds like crazy fun, and it is! You can go as wild as you like with glam – this look is all about exaggeration!

STARDOLL DICTIONARY

Glam rock: *1. A style of rock music that became popular in the early seventies. 2. A fashion trend inspired by the flamboyant stage outfits of the glam rock scene.*

This silver stripy print screams seventies disco cool!

Go back in time with pirate-inspired accessories.

10, 9, 8, 7, 6, 5, 4, 3, 2, 1 . . . lift off in space-high platforms!

Over this way for more glam rock!

When you're choosing your glam rock colours and fabrics, take it to extremes! Silver, gold, sequins . . . this trend needs some serious stardust! But the shine-factor doesn't have to stop there. Try accessorising with glossy patent boots, belts and bags. Feathers and ruffles are another big part of this trend. Picture a highwayman, a pirate and a spaceman at a clothes swapping party and you'll have the right idea! Get your glam on, girl!

Get the style groove with seventies-inspired colours.

Think theatrical, with flamboyant, historical shades.

Look out for funky patterns and prints!

MEDOLL STYLE

You're going to need sequins and metallics for this look, so search your wardrobe for all that glitters. Go for fitted clothes with a seventies vibe and finish the look with patent platforms!

HOW TO DO CASUAL

The secret to looking fabulously casual is to dress in designs that look relaxed, chilled and totally stylish. You know those pictures you see of celebs walking their dogs? That's casual styling at its best! Go for jeans, shirts, cute little tees, fine-knit cardigans, sporty sweatshirts and anything with a laid-back vibe. Accessories range from cool scarves to oversized bags and cute hats. Think chilled, and style it up anyway you like!

STARDOLL DICTIONARY

Casual: *1. Informal, untailored clothes that are comfy, cool and relaxed. 2. Having a carefree and relaxed attitude.*

These slouchy shorts get the casual trend spot on.

A soft leather bag adds a touch of casual colour.

Don't you just love the way the shoes pick out the pink on the bag?

Turn over the page for some casual colours!

Casual clothes come in all the colours of the rainbow, from pillar-box red to pretty pastels. Pick one main colour for your base and then build the rest of your outfit around it. Cotton, linen and jersey are perfect for casual tops, skirts and dresses. The secret is to pick out fabrics that feel relaxed and comfortable. Prints and patterns are HUGE in casual wear, so go crazy with ditzy florals, stripes, cute prints and anything else that catches your eye!

Rainbow bright colours and pretty pastels.

Denim, jersey, linen and cotton have all got casual appeal.

Choose any kind of print and pattern you like!

MEDOLL STYLE

Style up your MeDoll's jeans or leggings with a cute top and some super-casual accessories, or go for a pretty dress or skirt. Just think laid-back, chilled-out cool!

HOW TO DO BOHO

The chilled-out boho trend was inspired by styles from the sixties and seventies. Laid-back layers and natural fabrics are a key part of the look. Go with the flow in floor-sweeping maxi dresses, swishy mini dresses, gypsy skirts, denim and leggings. Team separates with tops, tunics and shirts that are printed or plain. Then finish off with leather belts, fringed waistcoats, beads and bangles. Feel that boho vibe, baby!

STARDOLL DICTIONARY

Boho: 1. A laid-back trend inspired by natural fabrics, ethnic prints from around the world and the hippy vibe of the sixties and seventies. 2. Boho is short for bohemian.

The retro seventies hat tops off the look!

Fringing is a big hit with boho babes.

Work boho to the max with a ditzy print dress.

Turn over the page for plenty of boho patterns!

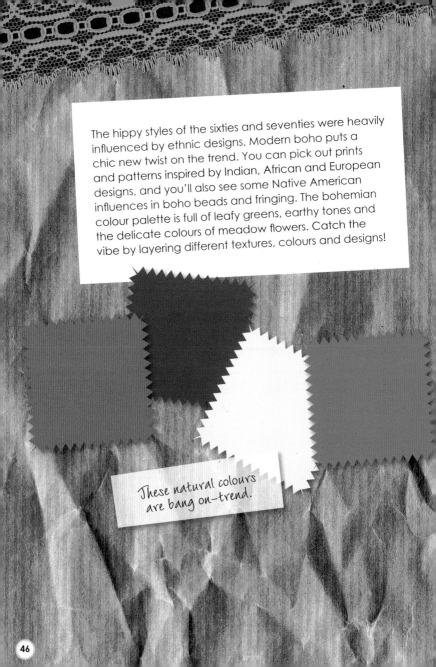

The hippy styles of the sixties and seventies were heavily influenced by ethnic designs. Modern boho puts a chic new twist on the trend. You can pick out prints and patterns inspired by Indian, African and European designs, and you'll also see some Native American influences in boho beads and fringing. The bohemian colour palette is full of leafy greens, earthy tones and the delicate colours of meadow flowers. Catch the vibe by layering different textures, colours and designs!

These natural colours are bang on-trend.

Look out for boho
details and textures.

Pick prints and patterns
from around the world.

MEDOLL STYLE

Get the boho look for your MeDoll with just few key
items. A long maxi dress, a crocheted waistcoat,
printed leggings and a tunic will get you on track.
Ooh, and don't forget your boho accessories!

HOW TO DO PREPPY GEEK

If you get preppy geek right, you'll look clever and classy all at the same time! Start off with some classic preppy pieces – look out for shirt dresses, cotton skirts, chinos and polo shirts. Now style it up with some traditional geeky touches. We're talking white socks, computer-print tees, smart ties and oversized glasses. Do it if you dare!

STARDOLL DICTIONARY

Preppy Geek: *1. A look that's smart, stylish and kinda quirky. 2. The word preppy was originally used to describe students who went to university preparatory schools in America.*

A cute cardigan is a preppy geek essential.

Preppy geeks love wearing plain colours.

An oversized bag totally completes the look!

Turn over the page for more preppy geek!

There are three main groups of preppy geek colours – pretty pastels, brilliant brights and geeky shades of brown and tan. The contrast is pretty wide, so keep co-ordinated when you're putting your look together. Clothes and prints inspired by tennis and sailing are huge for preppy geeks, so look out for boat-necked sweaters, v-necked tees, oxford shirts and pleated tennis-style skirts. Think nice, think neat, think preppy geek!

Pretty pastels are bang on-trend.

Chill out in bright,
sporty colours.

Pick patterns inspired
by school and sports.

MEDOLL STYLE

If you've already got some basic block colours in
your wardrobe, you're nearly there! Just style up your
look with a blue blazer, a tie or a geeky print t-shirt.

HOW TO DO PRETTY

Forget dark colours, graphic prints and tailored designs – the pretty look is all about soft fabrics, princessy cuts and delicate fairytale colours. Dress it up with floaty skirts, gorgeous gowns, fifties-inspired dresses and elegant harem pants. Dress it down with ballet cardigans, pretty printed t-shirts and cute skinny jeans. You can wear this look every day!

STARDOLL DICTIONARY

Pretty: *Bows, butterflies, ballet, ribbons, ruffles, flowers, lace, gems and anything else that's gorgeously girly!*

This petal-pink dress is so princess pretty.

Use silky or satiny fabrics for that fairy queen feel.

Add nature-inspired details to your accessories.

There are more pretty palette ideas on the next page!

When it's time to choose your pretty colours, patterns and prints, let your inner princess go wild! Look around for inspiration and pick out the prettiest shades you can find. Go for pretty pales and 'barely there' tints of blue, yellow, pink and lilac. Think ballet, cupcakes, petals, butterflies and fairies! Dresses and skirts are a natural choice, but you can work the pretty look in your jeans, too. Just pair them with shimmery tops, lace trimmed vests or sweet printed t-shirts. The choice is yours!

Ballet-inspired colours are big in this trend.

MEDOLL STYLE

Head to the Fashion Design studio and create the prettiest fabric ever! Choose a cute top or shirt pattern that you can team with a floaty skirt or your MeDoll's favourite jeans.

HOW TO DO QUIRKY

If you love cute, unusual clothes and accessories, you'll love trying out this look! Quirky girls like fashion that expresses their individuality. Vintage skirts, tops and accessories are great for this trend, and there are plenty of quirky clothes on the high street, too. Add your own cheeky little twist to the trend. Get quirky!

These necklaces are unusual and totally quirky-cool.

The quirky cut of the bubble skirt means it stands out from the crowd.

Really rock the look with layers of long-length socks!

Turn over the page for some quirky colours!

When it comes to choosing your quirky palette, it's all down to the way you feel. Pick a crazy mish-mash of clashing colours, choose vintage-inspired tones or make a statement with just one bold colour. Pick out unusual patterns, prints and textured fabrics. Look at the shape of clothes, too – if the cut of a garment is unusual, it doesn't matter if it's plain or patterned! Where you take this look is up to you, so go for the styles you love!

Put a quirky spin on vintage colours.

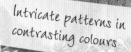

Intricate patterns in contrasting colours

Go all-out quirky in your texture choices.

MEDOLL STYLE

Chunky beads, statement pendants, vintage brooches, hats . . . Accessories are such a key part of this trend, so have fun picking out some unusual pieces at the StarBazaar.

59

HOW TO DO METALLICS

Parties, proms, sparkling celebrations . . . Metallics are great for glamorous events. No wonder they're so popular on the red carpet! There are heaps of takes on this trend, from cascading gowns to shimmering leggings and spacey little jumpsuits. Go low-key in a t-shirt with a metallic print, or go totally crazy in head-to-toe shimmer!

STARDOLL DICTIONARY

Metallics: *Shimmery fabrics in shades of silver, gold, bronze and pewter.*

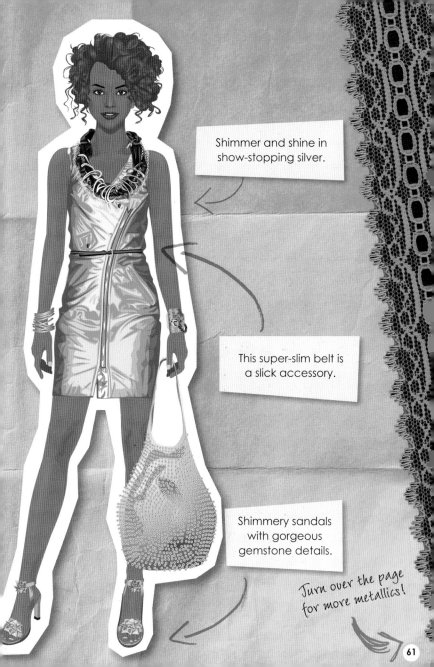

Shimmer and shine in show-stopping silver.

This super-slim belt is a slick accessory.

Shimmery sandals with gorgeous gemstone details.

Turn over the page for more metallics!

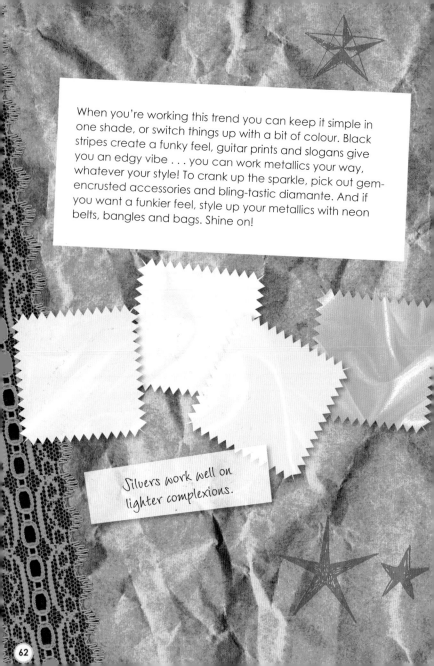

When you're working this trend you can keep it simple in one shade, or switch things up with a bit of colour. Black stripes create a funky feel, guitar prints and slogans give you an edgy vibe . . . you can work metallics your way, whatever your style! To crank up the sparkle, pick out gem-encrusted accessories and bling-tastic diamante. And if you want a funkier feel, style up your metallics with neon belts, bangles and bags. Shine on!

Silvers work well on lighter complexions.

Golds are gorgeous on darker skin tones.

Stand out and sparkle in textured fabrics.

MEDOLL STYLE

If you're dressing your MeDoll for the daytime, keep it subtle in a metallic print top. Then when night falls, go for a sparkling floor-length gown with matching accessories. Gorgeous!

HOW TO DO FESTIVAL

Festival style is a crazy mix of rock 'n' roll, preppy geek, chic and boho! The style started back in the sixties in the festival fields of America and England. Layering is a huge part of the trend and that's for practical reasons, as well as for style. When you're camping out, you need to be prepared for all kinds of weather!

STARDOLL DICTIONARY

Festival: *A chilled-out, summery look that's inspired by music festivals.*

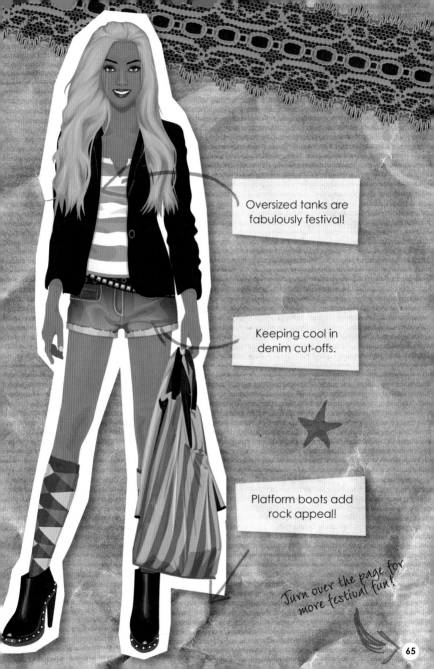

Oversized tanks are fabulously festival!

Keeping cool in denim cut-offs.

Platform boots add rock appeal!

Turn over the page for more festival fun!

Most festivals are on in the summer months, so sunshine trends rule. Cut-off denim shorts, cute hotpants, short skirts and dresses are a huge part of the festival look. Boho-influenced waistcoats and tunics are always popular, and maxi dresses are the height of festival chic! When it comes to accessories, you can take your pick. Go for sparkly gems, printed scarves, flowery headbands – the choice is yours!

Sunshine colours for that festival feeling!

Mix up different festival fabrics.

Hippy patterns and music-inspired prints.

MEDOLL STYLE

Start with boho trends as your base, then mix in some geeky little touches. Style your MeDoll in classic denim cut-offs, add a geeky waistcoat, a trailing scarf and a pair of flip-flops.

WHAT'S YOUR FASHION FORECAST?

Start here

How would you spend 1,000 Stardollars?
- New suite
- New clothes

What would you rather do today?
- Go out
- Chill out

What's the best plan for tonight?
- Dance party
- Girls' night

Pick what you'd rather do later.
- Cinema
- Internet

Which pet would you pick for your MeDoll?
- Puppy
- Pony

What would you rather do for lunch?
- Restaurant
- Picnic

Not sure what to wear? Just follow the arrows to reveal the styles that'll suit your mood.

What kind of singer would you rather be?

Sophisticated solo

A

Creative pop star

Talking

How would you express yourself right now?

B

Performing

Paris

Makeover

Where would you go on your dream holiday?

Which birthday surprise would you love?

C

Barbados

Sleepover

Hobby

What's the best way to spend the next few hours?

Turn over for the verdict

DVDs

THE VERDICT

A

FASHION FORECAST: A perfectly polished look would fit your sophisticated mood!

GET INSPIRED
- Make an impact in statement colours.
- Add glam with metallic accessories.
- Go for a side pony or a gorgeous up-do.

B

FASHION FORECAST: You're feeling pretty creative today, so get expressive with your style!

GET INSPIRED
- Express yourself with prints and patterns.
- Layer your jewellery for a quirky vibe.
- Fix your hair with some super-cute clips.

C

FASHION FORECAST: When you're feeling this relaxed and casual, laid-back styles are so your thing!

GET INSPIRED
- Relax in clothes that feel soft and stylish.
- Keep it casual with chunky jewellery.
- Wear your hair loose and tousled.

The ⭐ stardoll™ guide to personal style

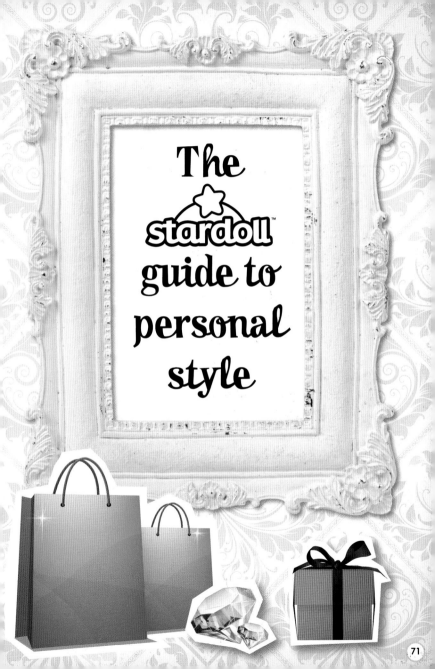

Style tips from the stars

It doesn't matter if you're crazy about sequins, sweatpants or street style, just get out there and express yourself, Stardolls!

You wear the look, don't let the look wear you. It's all about having self-confidence, which helps you pull off anything.

Katy Perry

Style to me is what makes you feel comfortable.

Jessie J

I'm just trying to change the world, one sequin at a time.

Lady Gaga

I love sweatpants! I own so many!

Selena Gomez

Don't do what everyone else is doing – remember what suits you rather than what someone else looks like in an outfit. You need to feel comfortable and get your own thing going on.

Fearne Cotton

Fashion is my way of expressing myself.

Emma Watson

Discover your Stardoll colours

Check out the pictures and pick the skin colour, hair colour and eye colour that's nearest to your own. Note down the flower that's next to your choices, then check out your Stardoll colours!

Do your colours first, and then take the test again for your MeDoll! How do your colours compare?

What colour is your skin?

What colour is your hair?

What colour are your eyes?

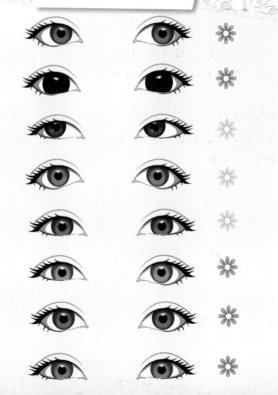

The verdict

Are you fresh, fierce or fabulous? Count up your flower score and then check your Stardoll colours!

Pssst! If you ended up with one of each flower, you can choose whichever colour wheel you like best!

Mostly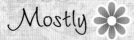

You're fresh!

All these light, fresh colours look gorgeous on you. Take your pick!

Cool, natural colours look just lovely against your skin.

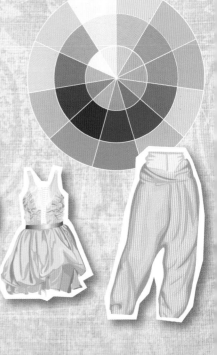

Mostly

You're fierce!

You've got what it takes to carry off a totally fierce, deep colour palette!

Jewel-bright colours look awesome with your complexion.

Mostly

You're fabulous!

You look totally fabulous in soft, bright sunshine colours. Get choosing!

Warm, summery shades look beautiful with your colouring.

How to build with basics

If you want to be truly stylish, you need to get your basics right. Here's how . . .

CUTE ALERT!

Your basics can be as cute and exciting as you like, just as long as the colours are plain. Focus on the shape of the garment and the quality of the fabric. Go for basics that say something to you and about you.

CLASH-O-RAMA DRAMA!

Imagine if all your tops and skirts had patterns on them. You'd have a serious case of clash-o-rama on your hands! Plain, basic tops, tees and jumpers are all essential when you're styling up your look, and so are basic trousers, jeans, skirts and dresses. Now, that's what you call fashion sense!

ACCESSORISE IT!

Basics bring out the best in your accessories! For instant chic, team a patterned scarf with a basic black top. Want a rocky look? Lose the scarf and add a studded belt. When you get the basics right, you can style up your outfit any way you want!

WHAT A GIRL NEEDS!

Great fitting jeans ✓
Leggings ✓
Jersey harem pants ✓
An above-the-knee skirt ✓
A white shirt ✓
A cute jumper ✓
Some t-shirts and vest tops ✓
A coloured dress ✓
A little black dress ✓
A blazer-style jacket ✓

STARDOLL DICTIONARY

Basics: *1. Simple, necessary things.*
2. Clothes you can mix and match to build loads of cool outfits.

MEDOLL BASICS

Head to the StarPlaza's Basics shop and pick up a few extra things. Now see how many new outfits you can create by mixing your new basics with the other clothes in your wardrobe! Can you build more than ten new looks?

79

How to ramp up your signature style

Do you and your MeDoll have the same signature style?

There's something about your style that makes you stand out from the crowd. Maybe your look is sporty or sophisticated? Maybe you're crazy about stripes or polka dots? Your signature style is all about the clothes, patterns and accessories that give you your own unique look. So ramp it up and get styling!

SUPER STYLING!

1. Add your signature touch to every outfit. Express yourself!

2. Go for bold or keep it subtle. Work your style, your way.

3. Keep mixing it up and trying out new signature looks.

> You have to be unique, and different, and shine in your own way.
> Lady Gaga

Signature style: *1. To have your own individual sense of fashion. 2. To express your personality with the clothes you love to wear.*

CELEBRITY SIGNATURES
Selena Gomez

Her look: Selena's style is so cute and casual! She keeps her look relaxed even when she's dressing up.
Steal her style: Sel loves flowery prints, so work those florals!

CELEBRITY SIGNATURES
Katy Perry

Her look: Katy's style is quirky and retro. She goes for super-cute details like polka dots and cherry prints.
Steal her style: Get Katy's look by working the polka dot trend!

CELEBRITY SIGNATURES
Lady Gaga

Her look: Lady G is a walking art gallery! She's always coming up with outrageous looks to surprise her fans.
Steal her style: Wear a totally crazy hat and act as if it's normal!

How to keep your clothes looking gorgeous

CARE LABELS

Care labels are sewn into the inside seams of your clothes and they have information on them to tell you how to wash your clothes. Some clothes need to be washed in cold water so they don't shrink, while other clothes can go through the hot wash. When you buy something new, check that crucial care label, so you know what to do!

JUST HANGING

If you've got any really delicate tops, using a padded coat hanger will protect them from damage.

HOW TO PACK A SUITCASE

First, put your shoes in a plastic bag and place it at the bottom of the suitcase, closest to the wheels. It makes your case easier to wheel if you put heavy stuff at the bottom!

Ok, so now you need to get your clothes in without creasing them. Lay your long-sleeved tops on the bed and fold the sleeves in toward the body. Fold the top in half from the bottom. Do the same with your jumpers and cardigans, then tackle your t-shirts.

Next, lay your skirts and trousers out and fold them all in half lengthwise. Stack them on top of your tops and put them neatly in your case.

Finally, put all your small stuff into little bags and use them to fill any gaps in your case. Now you're all set to jet set!

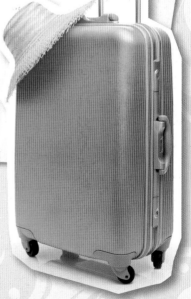

Shop like a personal stylist

TRY BEFORE YOU BUY

You can't tell what something will look like just by seeing it on a hanger . . . You need to get yourself in front of a mirror and fast, so head to the fitting rooms for a massive trying-on session! Check out the clothes from different angles, too – you don't want to end up with a skirt that looks great from the front and weird from the back! Use the back view and the side views, and if you're totally happy, go ahead and buy!

PERSONAL SHOPPING ASSISTANTS

Shopping is so much more stylish when you have your own assistant! If you have a little sister, why not invite her along to learn from your shopping expertise? She can help you carry your bags in return for the fabulous fashion lesson. Yep, that's what they call a win-win situation, people!

HOW TO BUY VINTAGE

If you want to grab a great vintage bargain, you need to be truly dedicated. Shopping for vintage stuff is totally different from shopping at high street stores. When it's vintage, chances are it's totally unique – so if you see something you love, snap it up before it goes!

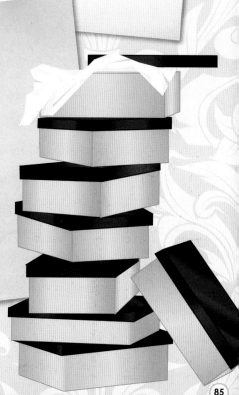

BAG A BARGAIN

Sales usually come around at the end of each season, and some shops have mid-season sales, too. If you know the sales are about to hit, head to the shops and try on all the things you like. Then when the sale starts, all you need to do is go back to the shop, pick what you like off the rail and head to the tills. You'll be gliding out the door with your bags while the other shoppers are still waiting for the fitting rooms. Nice work, style queen!

PLAZA TIME!

When you're shopping on Stardoll, think about how each new item will work with your other clothes and accessories. Oh, and picture the kind of shoes you need, too! It's the shoes and accessories that make your look unique.

To collect your exclusive Stardoll gift, go to www.stardoll.com and login or create an account. Then go to the Gift Card section under My Account and enter this code, before 31/12/2014: RH-JL742KQQE

What's your shopping style?

What kind of shopper are you?
Take this test to find out!

What would you do if you won a thousand Stardollars?

 Buy something special that you've had your eye on!

 Hit the Fashion Design studio to create your own designs.

 Splash out on a whole new wardrobe.

It's your best friend's birthday and you know she wants a new bag. Do you . . .

 Buy the most stylish bag you see without even checking the price.

 Give her a retro bag from a vintage shop. It's so unique, just like her!

 Hunt out a great bag store that's offering discount prices.

You're out in town with your BFs. What do you spend your money on?

 No idea! Your money just vanishes into thin air.

 A gorgeous top that you've been saving up for.

 Not much . . . just a milkshake to share with your friends.

You're in charge of decoration shopping for your little sister's party. How do you handle it?

 You ask if you can buy them online. It's cheaper than the shops!

 You get your BFs over to help you make some decs from scratch.

 You blow the budget on a roomful of helium balloons!

You're throwing a massive party on Stardoll. What's your outfit plan?

 Buy three new party outfits, just to be sure!

 Pick out something that's worth saving up for.

 Shop around and check out some prices.

The verdict

Mostly ★

Step away from the till, honey, people are beginning to stare! You don't need to buy everything in sight to prove you've got style! Get creative with the clothes you already have, focus on what you need and think before you buy!

Mostly ★

Just how do you manage to hunt out all the best deals 'n' discounts? You're just so awesome at tracking down the best deals, you must have been born with your own bargain-hunting radar! You rule the sale rails, Stardoll. Nice work!

Mostly ★

You love hanging at the shops with your BFs, but you're smart enough to keep your cash under control. When there's something you really want, you save before you splash! Girl, you're a savvy shopper, through and through!

Five
ICONIC
designers

ICONIC DESIGNERS

COCO CHANEL

Coco Chanel was born into a life of poverty and hardship, but her extraordinary talent and determination changed the course of fashion history . . .

Name:	Gabrielle Bonheur Chanel
Known as:	Coco Chanel
Nationality:	French
Life and times:	19th August, 1883 – 10th January, 1971
Signature styles:	Cardigan jackets, stripy Breton t-shirts and the famous little black dress.
Designer fact:	When Coco was 12, she went to live at a Roman Catholic orphanage. She was cared for by nuns, who taught her how to sew so that she could make a living as a seamstress. Little did they know that Coco would turn out to be one of the most iconic designers in history!

"A girl should be two things: classy and fabulous."

Coco Chanel

This pink suit has a classic cardigan jacket and is made from tweed — one of Chanel's favourite fabrics. The colours pink, black and white were a recurring theme in many of Coco's collections.

MARY QUANT

Mary Quant's clothes were made up of simple shapes, strong colours and bold patterns. Her cutting-edge designs changed the way girls dressed in the sixties . . .

Name:	Mary Quant
Nationality:	British
Life and times:	Mary was born on the 11th February, 1934.
Signature styles:	Mini skirts, patterned tights, hot pants and dresses with plastic collars.
Designer fact:	Mary Quant was one of the leading designers in the sixties. Before she arrived on the fashion scene, skirts were knee-length or longer. But girls kept asking Mary for skirts that were shorter and shorter, and that's how the mini skirt was invented! Mary named her skirt after her favourite car – the mini.

"Fashion as we knew it is over; people wear now exactly what they feel like wearing."

Mary Quant

Mary Quant wanted to design modern clothes that girls could easily move around in. Her little dresses were totally different to the longer styles that people had been wearing in the fifties. All the coolest girls were crazy about them!

95

VIVIENNE WESTWOOD

Vivienne Westwood is most famous for her shocking punk designs in the seventies. Her style has changed over the years, but her designs are just as exciting and unique . . .

Name:	Vivienne Westwood
Nationality:	British
Life and times:	Vivienne was born on the 8th April, 1941.
Signature styles:	Punky t-shirts, tartan prints, safety pins, studs and pirate-inspired fashion.
Designer fact:	Vivienne Westwood was part of the seventies punk movement. In 1971, she opened a shop on the Kings Road in London with her boyfriend, Malcolm McLaren, who was the manager of a punk band. She hung out with musicians and designed outrageous clothes that shocked the world!

"We based the look on rock 'n' roll right from the beginning."

Vivienne Westwood

As well as being inspired by music in her early career, Vivienne was also interested in traditional sewing techniques and fabrics. She even unpicked old clothes to see how they were made. She's famous for her original use of tartan.

ALEXANDER MCQUEEN

Alexander McQueen was famous for his spectacular catwalk shows. Lady Gaga, Sarah Jessica Parker and Rihanna have all been spotted in his designs . . .

Name:	Lee Alexander McQueen
Known as:	Alexander McQueen
Nationality:	British
Life and times:	17th March, 1969 – 11th February, 2010
Signature styles:	Skull prints, low-slung trousers, sharp tailoring and daring shoes.
Designer fact:	Lee McQueen began his fashion career when he was sixteen. He worked as an apprentice and mastered different tailoring techniques. After studying at college and working with other designers, he went on to set up a label under the name Alexander McQueen and won the British Designer of the Year Award four times.

"I get my ideas out of my dreams . . . if you're lucky enough to use something you see in a dream, it is purely original."

Alexander McQueen

Alexander McQueen was known for his unconventional approach to fashion. His clothes could be totally dramatic, like this black and red stripy dress, and his lavish catwalk shows were often theatrical and exciting.

MARC JACOBS

Marc Jacobs is one of the most admired designers in global fashion. His street-savvy designs have inspired fashion trends all over the world . . .

Name:	Marc Jacobs
Nationality:	American
Life and times:	Marc was born on the 9th April, 1963.
Signature styles:	Military jackets, fruit accessories, sharp tailoring and savvy street-wear.
Designer fact:	Marc Jacobs has earned the reputation for being one of the most versatile designers of our time. When he launches a new collection, the whole of the fashion world holds its breath! From grunge to gowns and immaculate suits, Marc Jacobs has a natural talent for designing clothes that people really want to wear.

"I love to take things that are everyday and comforting and make them into the most luxurious things in the world."

Marc Jacobs

Marc Jacobs is known for his ability to create clothes that are beautiful yet wearable. He designs dresses, skirts, trousers, suits and coats using sharp tailoring techniques. This cute short suit is relaxed and smart, all at the same time!

WHAT'S YOUR DESIGNER ID?

What kind of designer would you be? Take the quiz, then count up your coloured gemstones to reveal the truth!

Where do you wish you could buy your clothes in real life?

 Evil Panda

 Fudge

 Young Hollywood

Your MeDoll's going to a party. Where do you shop for an outfit?

 PPQ of Mayfair

 Wild Candy

 Killah

You're creating a fabric pattern in the Fashion Design studio. Which shape do you use?

 A star

A diamond

A lightning flash

If you could work in a Stardoll shop, which one would you choose?

 Voile

 Other World

 Rio

Which design would you sell at the StarBazaar?

 A rocky retro dress

 A gorgeous gown

 A smart shift dress

You're accessory shopping for your MeDoll. What do you pick?

 A plastic bangle

 A wide belt

 A printed scarf

You're throwing a party! Which room theme do you like best?

 Nightclub

 Wizards of Waverly Place

 Space

Turn over to reveal your designer ID!

THE VERDICT

Mostly 💎

You're cool and classic!
With your elegant taste and your eye for detail,
your gorgeous designs would be modern classics.
You'd be dressing stars like Emma Watson, Taylor
Swift and Cheryl Cole.

Most likely to design: Red carpet gowns, cute
tailored jackets and beautiful silk scarves.

Mostly 💎

You're fashion forward!
Your designs would light up the fashion world,
honey! With your awesome talent and imagination,
you'd be setting trends and dressing stars like Miley
Cyrus and Rihanna.

Most likely to design: Geometric skirts, shimmering
sequin dresses, floaty tops.

Mostly 💎

You're crazy quirky!
Your original take on design would have celebrities
racing to snap up your collection. You'd be brilliant
at designing imaginative stage outfits for superstars
like Katy Perry and Lady Gaga.

Most likely to design: Statement hats, miniskirts,
shimmery jumpsuits, retro skirts.

how to live life like an A-lister!

Think A-list!

YOU'RE A STAR

Who wants to waste their time being somebody they're not? True A-listers aren't afraid to live life by their own rules. Be yourself and be proud of everything you are – you're a star!

HIDDEN TALENT

Trying new things often reveals your hidden talents! That's why A-listers mix it up and grab as many opportunities as they can. What will you discover next time you do something different?

BEAUTY THERAPY

Being totally gorgeous takes effort, although most A-listers like to keep that a secret! Give your body the VIP treatment by eating well and exercising every day. You're so worth it!

ONLY THE BEST

It's all about quality, girls! Fill your life with all the best things – watch great TV shows, listen to the coolest music, eat healthy food and hang out with people who make you happy!

STYLE IT OUT

Style isn't just about fashion – it's a state of mind! A-listers stand tall and are proud of who they are. Put your own twist on style in real life, and on Stardoll. It's all up to you!

how to make an
A-list entrance

ARRIVING IN STYLE . . .

If you can't get your hands on a limo, don't panic! It's not the journey that matters here, it's the arrival. Walk up the drive, path or red carpet with your head high and your shoulders back. Think elegance, think confidence, think style! It's all about attitude, baby!

MEETING AND GREETING . . .

When you walk through the door, you'll want to head straight over to your BFs. But rushing past and ignoring other peeps could make your manners look totally Z-list! So say hello to people on the way in and then make your way towards your friends, oozing style and general awesomeness as you go. Good work!

DETAILS, DETAILS . . .

As you already know, putting on a party or event takes a heap of work, so let the host know that you appreciate their efforts. Earn extra style points by mentioning a few things you love about the event – the decorations, the food, the movie stars . . . It's good to notice the details!

CONGRATULATIONS, YOU'VE ARRIVED!

It's official! You are now fully qualified for red carpets, award ceremonies, celebrations and parties. Now get out there and greet your public!

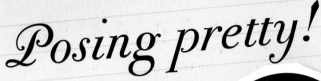

Posing pretty!

Strike a pose, A-listers! It's time for your close up . . .

THE HOLLYWOOD SMILE

The all-star Hollywood smile isn't just about lips and teeth – your eyes play a big part, too. Start by taking a deep breath and lowering your shoulders. Turn towards the camera, tilt your chin and smile as though you were about to laugh. Let the world see you sparkle, honey!

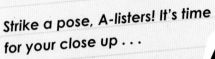

DO THE CELEBRITY TWIST!

1 As soon as you spy a photographer, turn partially sideways to the camera.

2 Place the foot closest to the camera slightly in front of your body.

3 Now rest your weight on your back foot and smile radiantly. Picture perfect!

MYSTERIOUS GIRL

Have you ever seen a picture of Leonardo da Vinci's 'Mona Lisa'? Her portrait is famous for having one of the most mysterious smiles in the history of lips! Stand in front of the mirror and try a half smile. Now try a quarter smile. OK, now smile a teeny-tiny bit less – yes, that's it! You've nailed the Mona Lisa smile, so now you can be as mysterious as you like!

First impressions

If you want to make a great first impression, show people the real you! Who wants to put on an act or pretend to be someone they're not? You're a true original, so be yourself and use your style and personality to dazzle the crowds from that very first moment!

Psssst! A-listers have been using this clever memory trick for years. When you're introduced to a big crowd of people, try saying each name three times in your head so you don't forget it.

Need a strategy to help you cope with awkward silences? Compliments and questions, people! That's the secret. Say how much you like somebody's shoes, ask about their job or their school, kick off the conversation with a friendly ice-breaker – you're bound to make a great impression!

Want to glow with confidence and charm? Flash that Hollywood smile and make loads of eye contact!

Let your style do the talking! Create your own First Impressions collection for you and for your MeDoll!

113

Five-star dinners!

This is what a formal table setting looks like . . .

Bread plate

Butter knife

Fish fork

Dinner fork

Salad fork

Soup bowl

WHAT'S WITH ALL THE FORKS?

Each course has its own cutlery. The waiter takes the used cutlery away after each course and you move onto a fresh set.

OUTSIDE IN!

Want to know which knife, fork or spoon you should use first? Go for the cutlery that's furthest away from your plate. Just start from the outside and work your way in. It's that easy!

WAITER ALERT!

Food is served from the left and drinks are served from the right. Watch your elbows, in case a waiter appears next you!

Dessert spoon

Dessert fork

Dinner plate

Soup spoon

Fish knife

Dinner knife

how to eat like an A-lister!

Want to dodge embarrassing dining disasters? Master the art of eating tricky food!

Spaghetti: Hold the fork down against your plate and twirl the spaghetti into a ball. Some people use a spoon under their forks to help with the twirling, but in Italy people just use forks.

Kebabs: Munching directly from the skewer is totally Z-list! Point the skewer towards your plate and use your fork to slide the food off the end. That's the A-list way!

Shared dips: Z-list alert! Putting something that's been in your mouth back into a shared dip is kinda gross. Whether you're dipping crudités (veggies!), pita or crisps, just dip once!

Olives: If they're in a bowl, use a spoon to put them on your plate, then pick them up and eat 'em with your fingers. Remove the pit with your fingers and put it on the side of your plate.

Tacos, wraps and fajitas: Pick them up with your hands and eat them as neatly as you can! If food falls onto your plate, just leave it to the end and eat it with your knife and fork.

The good gossip guide

Everyone likes catching up on the latest news, but what happens if gossip goes too far? How can you tell which gossip is good and which gossip is bad? There's a neat rule that A-listers use to help them decide. First imagine the person you're talking about, then imagine them reading what you're about to say on the front page of a newspaper. If you reckon they'd be upset, you know what to do!

One of my friends keeps repeating personal stuff about me. What should I do?

Talk to her about the way you feel. If she keeps gossiping, share your secrets with a friend you can trust instead.

Gossiping with your BFs is so much fun! But if a friend starts saying something you don't want to hear, just tell her to slow down. She probably just got carried away, but hey, you don't have to listen to bad gossip, right?

What's your A-list style?

What kind of celebrity would you be? Follow the arrows to find out!

Start here

Would you get lonely in a huge Hollywood mansion?

Maybe

Never

Are you the kind of person who can make a difference?

Absolutely

Hope so

Have you practised your red carpet walk?

So have

Not yet

Have you practised posing for the paparazzi?

So have

Not yet

Have you ever helped look after some little kids?

Totally

Not yet

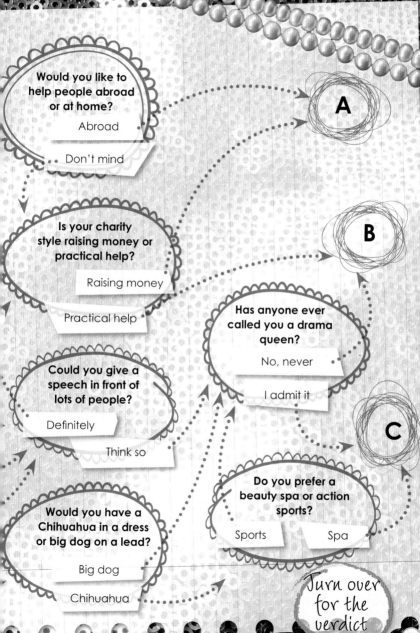

Would you like to help people abroad or at home?

Abroad

Don't mind

A

Is your charity style raising money or practical help?

Raising money

Practical help

B

Has anyone ever called you a drama queen?

No, never

I admit it

Could you give a speech in front of lots of people?

Definitely

Think so

C

Do you prefer a beauty spa or action sports?

Sports

Spa

Would you have a Chihuahua in a dress or big dog on a lead?

Big dog

Chihuahua

Turn over for the verdict

The verdict

Sweet charity
As well as being a totally talented celeb, you'd be completely caring, too! When you weren't busy working, you'd be raising money for charity and helping people all over the world. What a sweetie!

Totally inspired
You'd be the kind of celeb who'd want to help others achieve their dreams! You'd be dedicated to setting up special academies to help people improve their talents. What an inspiration!

Expert entertainer
You'd entertain the world with your crazy celebrity antics! You'd always be doing TV interviews and you'd probably insist that your dog had her own stylist. Tee-hee! What a drama queen!

How to have a natural spa

How to get the spa atmosphere

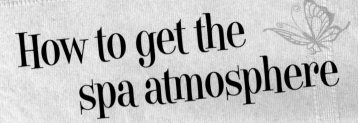

Want to turn your bedroom into a spa room? Here's how . . .

Whether you're relaxing with a face mask or enjoying a foot soak, it's always good to have your favourite magazines and books around! Collect a big pile together and have them close to your treatment area so you don't have to reach too far. Genius!

Ever noticed how music can completely change the mood? Some songs make you want to dance and some just make you want to kick back and relax! Choose your favourite chill-out songs to create your perfect pampering playlist. And if your BFs are coming over, get them to bring their spa sounds, too!

Music? Check! ✓

Magazines? Check! ✓

Now it's time to get your spa room smelling delicious!

Make a natural spa scent . . .

Sprinkle some rose petals into a bowl of warm water. Put the bowl in your spa room and the fragrance of roses will fill the air. No roses? No worries! Just use a slice of orange or lemon instead for a totally refreshing fragrance.

Try aromatherapy . . .

There are loads of different kinds of aromatherapy oils. Lavender oil is relaxing, so it's just right for a spa. Put two or three drops of oil in a bowl, add some warm water and your room will smell like a five star spa! Ahhhhhh!

Spa snacks

These tasty treats are bursting with beauty-boosting nutrients!

Fruit skewers

You'll need:

* fruit
* kebab skewers
* large plate

First choose your favourite combination of fruit. How about whole grapes, cubed mango and strawberries? Wash them and then carefully push your chosen fruit onto the kebab skewers. Finally, arrange them on a plate.

Blueberry cheesecake dip

You'll need:

⭐ 200g low-fat cream cheese

⭐ 1 tablespoon of honey

⭐ 50g blueberries

⭐ apple slices

⭐ bowl, fork, plate

Use a fork to mix the cream cheese, blueberries and honey together in a bowl. Put the bowl in the middle of the plate. Arrange the apple slices in a circle around the bowl and then get dipping!

Take care, Stardolls! Some foods can stain.

Pita bites

You'll need:

⭐ 1 wholegrain pita per person

⭐ mashed avocado

⭐ houmous

⭐ sliced cherry tomatoes

⭐ knife, plate

Carefully cut the pitas into thin strips. Spread half the strips with avocado and the other half with houmous. Then top all the pita strips with tomato and arrange them on a plate.

How to use your spa treatments

Savvy skin care

If you've ever read the back of a body lotion or face wash, you're bound to have seen the phrase 'Do not apply to broken skin'. That goes for all natural spa treatments as well as the stuff you buy in the shops. Skin that's sore or healing from a graze needs time to repair. If that's you, play it smart and avoid using treatments until you've healed.

Angel eyes

The area around your eyes is often more sensitive than the rest of your face. That's because the skin there is much thinner. Avoiding your eye area when you apply your face treatments will keep your skin smiling and your eyes safe.

Watch out!

Using your natural spa treatments in the bath or shower can make surfaces slippery. Take extra care when you stand up and clean everything after you've finished.

Best before

Use your natural spa recipes within 48 hours and store them in the fridge. They're best when they're fresh, people!

The beautician's patch test

Some skin treatments can trigger allergic reactions and make your skin feel sore. Before you use your natural spa treatment, dot a small amount on the back of your hand, cover it with a plaster and leave it for 24 hours. If your skin feels sore or itchy during your patch test, don't use the treatment!

129

VIP skin care

Follow this routine for spa-gorgeous-skin every day of the week! Wash your face with a gentle face wash twice a day and follow with a toner and moisturiser. Toners help to whisk away the last traces of oil and dirt from your skin and moisturising keeps your skin soft and hydrated. That's your daily skin care sorted, Stardolls!

TWICE A DAY

Toner

Pour a little toner onto a cotton pad, then gently sweep the pad across your face and neck in upwards strokes. Always avoid your eye area and never rub the cotton pad up and down.

TWICE A DAY

Moisturiser

Dot a small amount of moisturising cream onto the palm of your hand. Use the fingertips of your other hand to apply the moisturiser to your skin, taking care around your eye area.

ONCE A DAY

Facemask

Avoiding your eye area and lips, use your fingertips to spread a thin layer of the mask evenly over your skin. If you put it on too thickly, you could get it in your eyes or hair, so take care!

cream cleanser
NR 83

moisturiser
NR 102

How to make cucumber toner

You'll need:

* cucumber slices
* glass jar with a lid
* cotton pad

Put five slices of cucumber into a small jar. Fill up the jar halfway with water and leave it in the fridge for 20 minutes. While you're waiting, lay back and relax with a cucumber slice over each eye.

When your cucumber toner is ready, pour a little onto a cotton pad. Sweep the cotton pad over your face, taking care to avoid the area around your eyes. Now your skin is fresh and fabulous!

Why cucumber?

Cucumbers have calming properties and are naturally soothing to your skin.

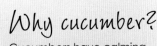

How to make apple toner

You'll need:

* apple quarter
* cheese grater
* glass jar with a lid
* spoon
* cotton pad

Carefully grate a quarter of a
small apple and spoon it into a jar.
Fill the jar halfway with water, then
stir the water and apple together.
Leave it in the fridge for 10 minutes and
the grated apple will sink to the bottom of
the jar.

Dip a cotton pad into the water at the top of the jar.
Sweep the cotton pad over your face, taking care to
avoid the area around your eyes.

Why apple?

Apples are packed with natural toners
which refresh and soften your skin.

How to make a honey face mask

You'll need:

⭐ 2 dessertspoons of dry porridge oats
⭐ 1 dessertspoon of natural yoghurt
⭐ 1 teaspoon of honey
⭐ small bowl
⭐ spoon

Put the oats, the yoghurt and the honey into a bowl and mix them all together. Cover the bowl and put the mixture in the fridge for 20-30 minutes.

Pat a thin layer of the mask onto your face, taking care to avoid the sensitive area around your eyes. Leave the mask on for 10 minutes, then rinse it off with water and pat your face dry with a clean towel.

Why honey, oats and yoghurt?

Honey contains natural moisturisers, oats are great for cleansing, and yoghurt helps to hydrate your skin.

How to make an avocado face mask

You'll need:

⭐ ¼ of a ripe avocado
⭐ 1 teaspoon of water
⭐ 1 teaspoon of honey
⭐ bowl
⭐ fork

Put the avocado in a bowl and mash it with a fork until it's smooth. Add the water and honey and mix everything together.

Using your fingertips, spread a thin layer of avocado mask over your face, avoiding your lips and eye area. Lay back and relax for 5 minutes, then wipe your face clean with a damp flannel and pat your skin dry with a towel.

Why avocado and honey?

Avocados are packed with healthy fats which help to moisturise your skin, and the honey gives your skin an extra hydration boost.

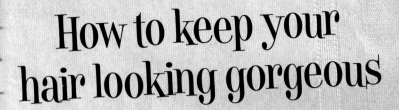

How to keep your hair looking gorgeous

Hair-healthy food!

Want your hair to grow quickly and healthily? It's time to tuck into some hair-friendly foods!

Carrots are a good source of vitamin A, which helps keep your scalp in great condition. Low-fat dairy products like milk and yoghurt are packed with a hair-friendly mineral called calcium. And fresh fruit, vegetables, nuts, salmon and pulses are also loaded with beauty boosting nutrients! Bon Appétit!

Say no to split ends!

Using conditioner regularly and having your hair trimmed every six weeks will keep split ends under control.

What's your hair type?

FINE HAIR: Use a gentle shampoo and a light conditioner. Oh, and go steady with styling products – they can weigh down your delicate hair.

MEDIUM HAIR: Use a gentle shampoo and conditioner for normal hair. Treat your hair to a natural hair mask every week to boost your shine factor!

THICK HAIR: Use a moisturising shampoo and conditioner. Make sure you double rinse, as your lovely, thick locks can hold in shampoo and conditioner!

CURLY HAIR: Use a conditioning shampoo and conditioner. Try using a shine spray to hydrate your curls, or try the olive oil treatment on page 138!

How to make an olive hair shiner

You'll need:

- ⭐ olive oil
- ⭐ towel
- ⭐ your usual shampoo and conditioner

Wrap a towel around your shoulders to protect your clothes. Put a few teaspoons of olive oil into the palms of your hands.

Start by massaging the oil into the roots of your hair. Keep working in small amounts of olive oil until all your hair is covered. Relax for 10 minutes, then shampoo and condition your hair as normal.

Why olive oil?

Olive oil nourishes and conditions your hair as well as improving its strength and elasticity. What's not to love?

How to make a banana hair mask

You'll need:

★ ½ a ripe banana
★ 1 tablespoon of honey
★ 1 tablespoon of olive oil
★ bowl
★ fork
★ towel
★ shampoo and conditioner

Put the banana, honey and olive oil into a bowl and mash together with a fork. Wrap a towel around your shoulders to protect your clothes.

Work the mask into the roots of your hair, then keep adding small amounts until all your hair is covered. Relax for 10 minutes, then just shampoo and condition your hair as usual.

Why banana, honey and olive oil?

The banana helps to control frizz, the honey hydrates, and the olive oil conditions and shines.

How to do a mani-pedi

Give your hands and feet a five-star treat!

Twinkle toes

1. Remove any nail polish and wash your feet with shower gel or soap.

2. Trim your toenails straight across the top with nail scissors or toenail clippers.

3. Treat your feet to your fave soak or scrub. Flip to the next pages to find the recipes!

4. Use a nailbrush to clean your toenails. Hold it at a 45 degree angle and brush gently.

5. Now use a pumice stone to gently smooth away any hard skin on your heels.

6. Rub your feet with body lotion, then add a thin layer of petroleum jelly over the top.

7. Slip on a pair of cotton socks while the lotion and petroleum jelly soften your feet.

*The word **pedicure** comes from the Latin word **pedis**, which means 'of the foot', and **cura**, which means 'care'.*

Happy hands

1. Remove any nail polish and wash your hands with a moisturising handwash.

2. Clean your fingernails with a nailbrush. Hold it at a 45 degree angle and brush gently.

3. If your fingernails are too long, trim them straight across the top with nail scissors.

4. Now use a nail file to shape your nails beautifully. File gently in one direction.

5. Brighten your fingernails and pamper your hands with the lemon soak on page 142.

6. Dry your hands, then rub a small amount of petroleum jelly around your cuticles.

7. Now use body lotion or hand cream to moisturise and condition your skin.

The word **manicure** comes from the Latin word **manus**, which means 'of the hand', and **cura**, which means 'care'.

How to make a lemon hand soak

You'll need:
- ⭐ 3 slices of lemon
- ⭐ warm water
- ⭐ bowl
- ⭐ towel

Fill a bowl halfway with warm water and add the lemon slices. Set the bowl aside for 10 minutes, then dip your nails in and soak them for 5 minutes.

Use a nail brush to gently clean your nails with the lemony water. Hold the nailbrush at a 45 degree angle and place the bristles under each fingernail. Move the brush gently from side to side. Rinse your hands and dry them with a towel

Why lemon?

Lemon juice contains natural acids, which will lighten and brighten your nails.

How to make a tropical foot soak

You'll need:

- ⭐ juice from a tin of pineapple
- ⭐ warm water
- ⭐ large plastic bowl or bucket
- ⭐ towel
- ⭐ pumice stone or exfoliating gloves

Fill a large plastic bowl or bucket with 7cm of warm water and add the pineapple juice. Put the bowl or bucket on a towel, to protect the floor from any splashes.

Soak your feet for 5 minutes, then gently rub your heels with a pumice stone or exfoliating gloves. Rinse your feet in clean water and dry them with a towel.

Why pineapple?

Pineapple contains a substance which naturally breaks down dead skin cells.

How to make a peach foot scrub

You'll need:

- ¼ of an overripe peach
- 70g sea salt
- 1 dessertspoon of olive oil
- bowl
- fork
- towel

Peel the skin off your peach quarter, put it in a bowl and use a fork to mash it into a fine *purée*. Add the salt and olive oil, then blend everything together with a fork.

Put a towel under your feet to protect the floor. Rub the scrub over your feet in circular movements. Rinse your feet and dry them with a towel.

Why peach, salt and olive oil?

Peach and olive oil hydrate your feet, while the texture of the sea salt smoothes away dead skin cells.

How to make a sugar foot scrub

You'll need:

⭐ 70g sugar
⭐ 1 dessertspoon of olive oil
⭐ bowl
⭐ spoon
⭐ towel

Put the sugar into the bowl and add the olive oil. Mix the ingredients together with a spoon.

Pssst! If you don't have any sugar, you can use sea salt instead!

Put a towel under your feet to protect the floor. Paying special attention to your heels, rub the sugar scrub over your feet in circular movements. Rinse your feet and dry them with a towel.

Why sugar and olive oil?

The olive oil softens and conditions your feet, and the texture of the sugar rubs away rough skin.

How to polish your nails like a pro

You'll need:

- ⭐ Nail polish remover
- ⭐ Hand soap
- ⭐ Nail file
- ⭐ Clear nail polish
- ⭐ Coloured nail polish

STEP ONE

If you want your polish to look totally pro, you need to start with clean hands and nails! Remove any traces of old nail polish. Wash your hands with gentle soap and pat them dry with a towel.

STEP TWO

Now use a nail file to shape your nails. Start from the left side and file towards the centre, then do the same on the right. File gently in one direction, and once the sides are done, file flat across the top.

STEP THREE

Before you use a coloured nail polish, paint a coat of clear nail polish on your nails. It helps protect your natural nail colour by stopping your nails from getting stained. Leave your nails to dry.

STEP FOUR

Pick out your colour and paint each nail in three sweeps. Start in the middle and sweep the brush towards the tip, then do the same on both sides. Leave them to dry and you're all set to go!

How to super-style your nails

The right nail design can really crank up your style! Match your nail colour to your outfit or just go for the clash effect – it's up to you! Try out some styles in the Starplaza and create your own unique look. Who says every nail has to be the same? Mix things up and push the limits!

Sketch out some designs in your notebook.

Brights and neons are super-hot right now!

SHINE ON!

Bare nail days don't have to be boring! On no-polish days, give your nails some natural shine with a quality nail buff.

Sparkly gems, cute designs . . . what's not to love?

WANT MODEL NAILS?

Keep painting and removing your nail polish and you could damage the natural beauty of your nails. Do what models do . . . choose a gentle nail polish remover and only use it once or twice a week. Disaster dodged!

TOP COAT!

Want to keep your nail colour looking gorgeous for longer? Just paint a coat of clear polish over your nails to give to them extra protection. Oh, but wait for your clear polish to dry before you get creative with your gems. Smudged is never a good look! Five minutes drying time should do it.

Reds and pinks scream sophistication!

How to do a French manicure

You'll need:

- ⭐ hand soap
- ⭐ towel
- ⭐ nail file
- ⭐ pale pink nail polish
- ⭐ white nail polish
- ⭐ clear nail polish

Want super-neat nails? The secret is not to overload your brush with polish.

STEP ONE

Remove your old nail polish. Wash your hands with moisturising hand soap and dry them with a towel. Now gently shape your nails with a nail file, filing in one direction.

STEP TWO

Paint your nails with your pale pink polish. Paint each nail with just three sweeps of the brush. Start in the middle of your nail, then paint the sides. Leave your nails to dry.

Smudged nails are not a good look! Relax for ten minutes between coats, to let your nail polish harden.

STEP THREE

Paint each white tip with one smooth stroke of the brush. You're only painting the tips of your nails, so you don't need much polish. Now wait for your tips to dry.

STEP FOUR

Paint your nails with a coat of clear nail polish. This layer of polish helps to protect your French manicure and make it look super glossy. Voilà! You are officially très chic!

How to get gorgeous nails

If you break a nail, trim it with a pair of nail scissors and file the edges smooth. Sorted!

Keep your cuticles soft and smooth by rubbing in a tiny drop of olive oil.

Vitamin A is great for nails! And there's lots of it in green veggies, cantaloupe melon and dried apricots, so get munching!

Rub hand cream into your hands and nails each night before you go to bed.

HAND LOTION

FACT!

If you had a nail-growing competition with your older sister, you'd probably win! The younger you are, the faster your nails grow!

FACT!

Nails are made of a hard protein called keratin. Your skin and hair also contains keratin. It's one of the important building blocks that make up your body.

How to host the best party ever!

The party plan

ming up an amazing party plan takes
, dedication and creative genius. So
e your checklist and start today!

Use this list to fire up some ideas and
add your own points as you go . . .

Party checklist

✓ Pick a fabulous party theme

✓ Send out super-stylish invitations

✓ Put together a dazzling outfit

✓ Organise a party playlist

✓ Put up party decorations

✓ Get snacks and drinks ready

✓ Clear an area for the dance floor

Have you had a Stardoll party yet?

THROW A STARDOLL PARTY!

Jump online, log on to Stardoll and choose a party room. Make it look gorgeous by dragging in your fave decorations. Now invite your BFs to your party by clicking on the 'friends' icon in the bottom menu. Find out more at www.stardoll.com

BEHIND EVERY GREAT PARTY IS A GREAT PARTY PLANNER!

WORLD'S BEST PARTY

Name your theme

Let's face it, themed parties are fully awesome! We're not talking kids stuff here, Stardoll party themes are all about style, sophistication and general fabulousness.

WHEN WE'RE FAMOUS

Get everyone to come as themselves when they're famous! Actors-to-be should come in red carpet outfits, future pop stars should wear stage costumes and tomorrow's show jumpers should dress in their jodhpurs . . . you get the picture!

POP STAR PARTY

Ask your mates to dress up as their fave girl bands, or throw your own Monsters' Ball and get your girls to wear costumes inspired by Lady Gaga. How many more pop-related party themes can you dream up?

MORE! MORE! MORE!

Throw a festival party and work the boho look.
Have a film wrap party and issue your mates
with VIP passes. Go nautical and decorate
your room like a yacht . . . What else can you
come up with?

PARTY IN
REAL WORLD
OR ON
STARDOLL!

Will the Stardoll Party rooms
inspire your real-world party?

Party shoe invitations!

Kick off your party in style with these super-cute shoe invitations!

STEP ONE

Place a thin sheet of paper over the pink shoe picture. Trace the picture and cut it out to make a shoe template. Put the template over the pink card and draw around the edge. Now cut out the shoe shape from the card, to make your invitation.

STEP TWO

Use a pencil to help you tie a bow for your invitation. Wrap the ribbon around the pencil and tie it in a double knot. Tie the ribbon in a bow, then carefully push the bow off the top of pencil. Dab some glue on the double knot and stick the bow onto your invitation.

STEP THREE

Write your party details on your invitations. Write your guest's name at the top and then add the time and date of the party. If you're going to have a dress code or a party theme, make sure you include those details, too. Finally, decorate your invitation with gems, for that fabulous finishing touch!

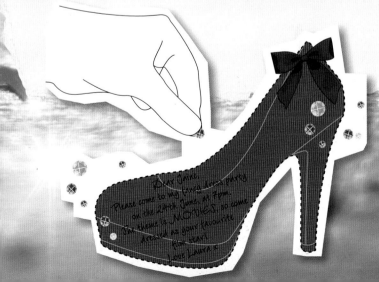

Dear Jane,
Please come to my fancy dress party on the 24th June, at 7pm. The theme is MOVIES, so come dressed as your favourite film star!
Love Laura x

Party trends

When it's time to party, crank up the style factor and express your individuality any way you want!

SHIMMER AND SHINE

Whether you go for a sparkly bracelet or a full-on sequined dress, nothing says party like a bit of sparkle! Tie the whole look together with some seriously glittery nail polish and shine on!

CLASSIC SOPHISTICATION

Ever since Coco Chanel invented the little black dress, it's been a party classic. Add a shot of colour to your LBD with a neon belt or a pair of coloured shoes. Très chic, chérie!

LAID-BACK COOL

If you're crazy about denim, combats or leggings, simply style them up with shimmery tops and show-stopping accessories. Do party fashion on your own terms and rock the laid-back look!

Shoulder pads give this outfit a strong, structured feel.

The shimmery fabric of this jacket screams party glamour.

See how the cream edging on the boots matches the shirt and skirt? Nice detailing!

Party food

Your guests will go crazy for these delicious snacks!

SWEET CHILLI BITES

You'll need:
- ⭐ mini crackers
- ⭐ cream cheese
- ⭐ sliced cherry tomato
- ⭐ ham
- ⭐ sweet chilli sauce

Spread a layer of cream cheese onto a cracker, add a slice of tomato or ham and drizzle with sweet chilli sauce. Use houmous instead of cream cheese if you like!

PARADISE ON A STICK

You'll need:
- ⭐ melon balls
- ⭐ desiccated coconut
- ⭐ grated chocolate
- ⭐ cocktail sticks

Mix the chocolate and coconut together in a bowl. Roll a melon ball in the mixture until it's coated. Push the cocktail stick through the melon and serve.

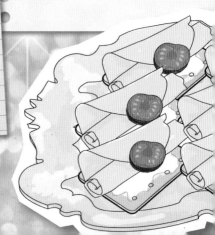

HONEY NUT ROLLERS

You'll need:
- ★ wholemeal wrap
- ★ peanut butter
- ★ honey

Spread a wholemeal wrap with a thin layer of honey and peanut butter. Roll the wrap as tightly as you can, then cut it into bite-sized strips.

SUMMER SKEWERS

You'll need:
- ★ strawberries
- ★ melon cubes
- ★ small kebab skewers

Push a melon cube onto a kebab skewer and follow it with a strawberry. Add another melon cube and strawberry to complete your snack.

The party countdown!

24 HOURS TO GO

When you're throwing the perfect party, you need the perfect party outfit! Avoid last minute fashion disasters by getting everything ready now. With 24 hours to go, there's loads of time if you need to wash your favourite top or go shopping for some new accessories. Phew!

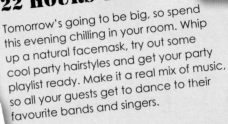

22 HOURS TO GO

Tomorrow's going to be big, so spend this evening chilling in your room. Whip up a natural facemask, try out some cool party hairstyles and get your party playlist ready. Make it a real mix of music, so all your guests get to dance to their favourite bands and singers.

8 HOURS TO GO

Drum roll, people! It's time to decorate your party room! Go subtle with a few fairy lights or unleash a full-on party theme. Once you've nailed the decorations, take care of the practical stuff. Crack out some coasters and move any breakable ornaments out of your dancefloor area!

3 HOURS TO GO

Listen up, this is the serious bit! It's time to brief your parents. Under no circumstances are they allowed to join in karaoke or demonstrate the dance moves of their youth. In return for their good behaviour, let them have some party snacks, so they don't feel too left out!

1 HOUR TO GO

Woo hoo! It's time to get ready! Since your outfit is already sorted, you can spend ages on your hair. Now you're looking gorgeous and you're all set to party! Head downstairs, lay out all your party snacks and wait for the doorbell to ring. It's going to be a brilliant night!

Ice breakers

Get your party started with these super-fun ice-breakers!

POSTER BOY

For this crazy ice breaker, you need a poster of a cute celeb boy, a scarf, paper, pens, scissors and some sticky putty. Get each guest to draw a pair of lips on the paper, then cut them out and add a ball of sticky putty to the back. Choose a party guest to go first and blindfold her with the scarf. She has to stick her paper lips on the poster as close to the celeb's lips as she can! Take it in turns and see who can get her lips the closest!

NAIL BAR

Grab loads of different coloured nail polishes and sit in a circle on the floor. Ask the girl on your right to spin one of the nail polishes in the middle of the circle. When it stops spinning, whoever the lid is pointing to must paint one of her nails with the polish. When she's finished, she chooses a new polish to spin. Yep, you guessed it. . . whoever the lid points to this time also gets to paint one of her nails and spin a new polish! Keep playing until everybody's nails are amazingly multi-coloured!

LADY GAGA'S STYLIST

For this ice breaker you need a pile of old newspapers and a roll of tape for each group. Ask your party guests to split into small teams and give each team a roll of tape and a pile of newspapers. Pick one person in each group to be Lady Gaga. The other team members must use the newspaper and tape to create an outfit for her! The only rule is that you can't stick tape to clothes, hair or skin. (D'uh, as if you'd want to do that anyway!) As the host, you get to decide which Lady Gaga outfit is the most outrageous!

RED CARPET FREEZE

Ok, party people! This ice breaker taps into your acting abilities, so get ready to put on a performance! Grab a camera, pick one guest to be the photographer and one guest to be the DJ. Everyone else is a celebrity. When the DJ plays the music, the celebs must act as if they're walking up a red carpet, posing like crazy. When the DJ stops the music, the celebs must freeze while the photographer snaps some photos. Hee-hee! Those pictures are gonna be awwwesome!

What's your party personality?

Want to reveal your party ID? Just follow the arrows to discover the truth!

START

What's the best reason to throw a party?

- Birthday
- Holiday

How long does it take you to get dressed for your party?

- Less than an h[o...]
- Over an hou[...]

Whose songs would you rather sing at karaoke?

- Selena's
- Rihanna'[s]

Which band would get you dancing?

- The Saturdays
- JLS

How would you help your guests get to know each other?

- Ice-breaker games
- Crazy karaoke

172

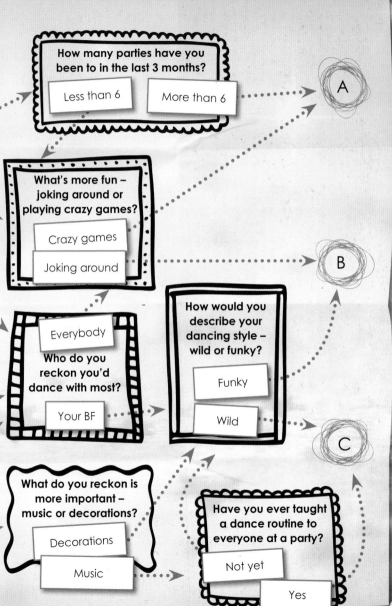

How many parties have you been to in the last 3 months?

Less than 6

More than 6

What's more fun – joking around or playing crazy games?

Crazy games

Joking around

Everybody

Who do you reckon you'd dance with most?

Your BF

How would you describe your dancing style – wild or funky?

Funky

Wild

What do you reckon is more important – music or decorations?

Decorations

Music

Have you ever taught a dance routine to everyone at a party?

Not yet

Yes

A

B

C

173

The verdict

A

YOU'RE A PARTY PRO!

No wonder you get invited to so many parties, honey! You're a complete professional! You know all the best ice-breaker games and you're great at getting everyone chatting. Nice work!

B

YOU'RE A PARTY PRINCESS!

Not only are you a totally talented host, you're also a brilliant guest! You know exactly what makes a party rock and you always get everyone laughing and dancing. You're party royalty!

C

YOU'RE A PARTY ANIMAL

Music is a big part of the party scene and that's where you come in, girl! You know all the best party tunes and you're a pretty wild dancer, too. You're a party animal, through and through!

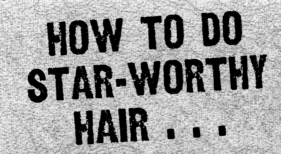

HOW TO DO STAR-WORTHY HAIR . . .

HOW TO FIND YOUR PERFECT HAIRSTYLE

PSSSST! THE SHAPE OF YOUR FACE CAN MAKE SOME CUTS AND STYLES LOOK FABULOUS!

WHAT'S YOUR SHAPE?

Working out your face shape can be pretty tricky. You may not fit into one category exactly, so look for similarities rather than a perfect match. If you're not sure where to start, tie your hair back and look into a steamed up mirror. Use your finger to trace the reflection of your face in the steam. Which shape does it look like most – oval, round, rectangular or heart-shaped?

OVAL LIKE KATY PERRY

So right: Just like Katy, your face shape suits almost every sort of hairstyle. You guys are so lucky!

So long: Extra-long hair could swamp your pretty features.

RECTANGULAR
LIKE CHERYL COLE

So right: A crop, a quiff and a fringe are just some of the styles that make you and Cheryl look fab!

So long: Blunt cuts aren't your thing. Go for wispy layers.

ROUND LIKE
LADY GAGA

So right: You and Lady Gaga have loads of style options. Quiffs and ponys will always look awesome!

So long: The chin-length bob is not your friend!

HEART-SHAPED
LIKE SELENA GOMEZ

So right: Choices, choices! Swishy cuts, glam up-dos and wavy layers all look cute on you and Sel!

So long: Super-short boy cuts can be hard for you to wear.

Head over to www.stardoll.com and play around with different hairstyles and face shapes. Which hairstyles work best for you and your MeDoll?

177

STYLE YOUR HAIR LIKE YOUR MEDOLL!

LAID-BACK UP-DO

You'll need:

* Hairbrush
* Bobby pins or a hair claw

1 Brush the tangles out of your hair. Gather your hair together as if you were going to put it into a low ponytail. No need to use a hair elastic, just hold it in place with your hand.

2 Use one hand to hold your ponytail in place at the base. Now use the other hand to twist your pony in a clockwise direction. Gently pull it upwards as you twist.

3 Keep twisting until all your hair is loosely coiled. Hold the coil against your head. Use a hair claw to fix it in place near the top of the coil, or some bobby pins.

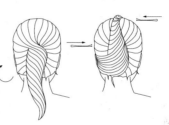

4 Now gently tease out a few tendrils of hair at the top of the coil, so they hang down prettily. If they're sticking up too much, loosely twist each tendril for a more laid-back look.

STYLE YOUR HAIR LIKE YOUR MEDOLL!

GORGEOUS WAVES

You'll need:
* Hairbrush
* Hair elastics

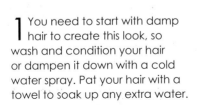

1 You need to start with damp hair to create this look, so wash and condition your hair or dampen it down with a cold water spray. Pat your hair with a towel to soak up any extra water.

2 Comb your damp hair so it's tangle free, then style it into a side parting. Take a little section of hair next your parting, plait it all the way down and secure it with a hair elastic.

3 Now do the same on the other side of your parting with an equal amount of hair. Keep plaiting your hair evenly on both sides. (Even plaits stop your waves from being lopsided!)

4 Leave your hair to dry, then undo your plaits. Brushing your hair could make your new waves fall out, so use your fingers to smooth and style your hair instead. Beach babe gorgeous!

STYLE YOUR HAIR LIKE YOUR MEDOLL!

POP STAR QUIFF

You'll need:
* ⭐ Hairbrush
* ⭐ Bobby pins

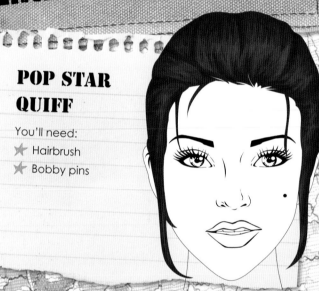

1 Brush the hair at the front of your head forward. Take a v-shaped section of hair from your forehead to your crown. This front section of hair will become your pop star quiff!

2 Hold the front section of your hair up in the air. Starting at your forehead, brush it upwards to smooth it out. This will make your finished quiff look neat and even from the front.

3 Now loosely twist the front section of your hair three times. If you want a lower quiff, try a tighter twist. Everybody's hair is a bit different, so just do what works for you!

4 Push the twist of hair slightly forward and check your look in front of the mirror! Once you like what you see, secure your quiff in place with bobby pins. You've got the style!

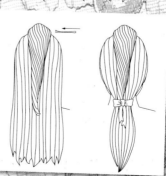

STYLE YOUR HAIR LIKE YOUR MEDOLL!

CHIC CHIGNON

You'll need:

- ★ Hairbrush
- ★ Comb
- ★ Hair elastics
- ★ Bobby pins

1 Brush the tangles out of your hair and put it into a ponytail halfway up your head. Now use your finger and thumb to take hold of the top half section of your ponytail.

2 Tuck the ends of the top section around your forefinger and roll your hair inwards around your finger, until you reach your head. Use bobby pins to fix the roll over the top of your pony.

3 Now take hold of the bottom half of your ponytail. Roll your hair as you did before, but this time, roll it down towards your neck. Use bobby pins to fix it underneath your ponytail.

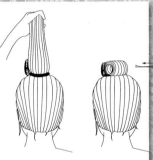

4 Slowly ease out the edges of your rolled hair so the loops form a circle around your ponytail elastic. Fix your style with bobby pins, then add some sparkly gems. Ta-daa!

HOW TO DO THE NEW PONYTAILS

THE PONYTAIL WRAP

Put your hair into a high ponytail and hold it in place with a hair elastic. Take roughly a sixth of your ponytail and wrap it around the hair elastic until it's totally covered. Now fix the ends of the wrapped section underneath your ponytail with a bobby pin. Easy!

THE PONY QUIFF

Take a v-shaped section of hair from the front of your head. Loosely twist it, then push the twist slightly forward to make a quiff and secure it in place with bobby pins. Now put your hair into a sky-high pony and use a metallic hair elastic to hold it in place. Street stylin'!

THE SIDE PONY

Sweep your hair over to one side to create a loose side ponytail. Fix it in place with a hair elastic, just below your ear. Now all you need to do is pick a hair accessory! Go tropical with a flower garland or crank up the glamour with a sparkly clip. Get ready to dazzle!

SELENA GOMEZ LOVES WEARING A PONYTAIL! "IT MAKES ME FEEL SOPHISTICATED," SHE SMILES.

THE LAIDBACK PONY

Brush your hair back with your hands and secure it at the nape of your neck with a hair elastic. Leave some tendrils of hair free around your face to frame it prettily. Wrap a length of lacy ribbon around your hair elastic, tie it in a knot and leave the ends loose. So cute!

WHAT'S YOUR HAIRSTYLE ID?

What does your 'do say about you? Tick one box for each question, then work out your score to reveal your hairstyle ID!

You're styling your MeDoll for her winning Cover Girl picture. Which hairstyle do you pick?

A tousled style ☐

A glam chignon ☐

A laid-back look ☐

You're going to be a bridesmaid next Saturday. What's your essential hair accessory?

A sparkly tiara ☐

Cute hair gems ☐

A pink rose ☐

Your school's having a prom! Your dress is sorted but how are you going to wear your hair?

Loose and lovely ☐

Celeb-worthy up-do ☐

A super-cute quiff ☐

It's party time for your MeDoll! What hairstyle do you choose at the Beauty Parlour?

Dramatic curls ☐

A pixie crop ☐

Natural waves ☐

If you could steal a star's hair for the day, whose would you choose?

Zendaya Coleman ☐

Taylor Swift ☐

Selena Gomez ☐

You're on a family camping trip. What do you use to keep your hair looking sweet in the great outdoors?

A pink headband ☐

A sophisticated clip ☐

A pretty ponytail ☐

Step into the spotlight, girl! You're famous! Choose your red carpet hair accessory.

A diamond-studded hair clasp ☐

A stylish silk flower ☐

A butterfly fascinator ☐

Turn over to reveal you hairstyle !

189

THE VERDICT

Mostly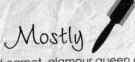

Roll out the red carpet, glamour queen coming through!
That's right, honey – with your dazzling style and extrovert
personality, you were born to turn heads!
Most likely to say: 'Who says a tiara isn't appropriate
school wear? That's crazy!'

Mostly

Wherever you are, whatever you're doing, you're always
as sweet as sugar! You love hanging out with your BFs
and talking clothes, pop and all things girly!
Most likely to say: 'Take it from an expert – you can never
have too much pink.'

Mostly

Girl, you're a true individual! You're not afraid to mix
things up and go wild. No wonder your friends are crazy
about your quirky take on life and fashion!
Most likely to say: 'Who wants to look the same as
everybody else? I've got my own style!'

It's all about You!

Treat yourself like a VIP

Are you ready to get glowing? Follow these tips and treat yourself to the best!

FLEX IT

Yoga is a big hit with celebs and if you haven't tried it yet, you're missing out! Yoga strengthens all the muscles in your body and helps keep you flexible. It's also great way to wind down and relax after a hectic day.

CHILLAX!

Stressing and rushing around all day is no fun at all! Make time to chill. Put on your favourite CD, design some clothes for your MeDoll or read a book – do whatever helps you to unwind.

DRINK UP

The human body is about 60%-70% water. That's right, girl, you're practically an ocean! Water transports oxygen and nutrients around your body, removes waste and protects your joints and organs. Drink at least 8 glasses of water a day to keep your body topped up!

JUST DANCE!

Dancing is a great way to get active! It sets your heart pumping and keeps your muscles strong. And the best thing about dancing is that you can do it on your own or with your BFs. What's not to love?

Turn the page to discover the secrets of beauty-boosting food!

Treat yourself like a VIP

For glowing skin, gorgeous hair and strong nails, eat at least one serving of protein every day. Lean meat, fish, eggs and pulses, like chickpeas and lentils, are all great sources of protein.

Vitamin A is famous for its beauty-boosting powers! Foods like carrots, sweet potato, mango and spinach all contain vitamin A, and so do eggs and fish.

Nuts and avocados are crammed with essential fats, vitamin E, and B vitamins. You need all these nutrients for healthy skin, hair and nails.

Fruit and vegetables contain vitamin C, which helps your body produce a skin-friendly substance called collagen.

Wholegrains are packed with fibre, which helps keep your digestion healthy and your skin clear. Get your boost from wholegrain bread and breakfast cereals.

ALLERGY WARNING!
If you're allergic to any of the beauty foods, don't eat 'em! Instead, look for other foods that contain the same nutrients.

The happy charts

AIM HIGH

You know that secret dream you have? The one where you imagine yourself doing something completely awesome? Whether your goal is big or small, start working towards it today. Build up your skills, perfect your talent and aim for the stars!

LOL!

Laughing out loud is good for you! Laughter relaxes your body and blasts away stress. So stick on your favourite comedy movie, joke around with your family or get giggling with your girls!

GET INSPIRED

Are you ready to get cheesy? Like really, reeeally cheesy? Ok, grab a notebook and make a list of all the things you feel happy about. Keep it in a secret place and get it out next time you need some happy inspiration!

The happy charts

GIRL TIME

Doing cool stuff puts juice in your happy tank! Get together with your BFs and plan something awesome! Form a band or put on a play, plan a party or a Stardoll fashion show, organise a fundraiser for your favourite charity – come up with some brilliant ideas and get ready for happy!

Show me the happy!

Use this list to fire up some ideas, then make a happy list of your own!

☐ Design a show-stopping outfit for your MeDoll.

☐ Give your dreams a whirl and become a Stardoll Stylist!

☐ Learn a new dance routine with your BFs.

☐ Make your own Star Movie and show your Stardoll friends!

☐ Make your friends LOL until they cry!

☐ Get totally awesome at your latest hobby!

☐ Throw a party on Stardoll and invite all your BFs.

☐ Head to the park and play sport with your buds!

The school of cool!

Let's face it, when it comes to being cool, you've already got it nailed. You've got the style, you've got the talent and you've got the attitude! If you were a stick of rock, you'd have cool written all the way through you!

SHAKE IT OUT

Being stressed can seriously damage your cool-o-meter. When you start to feel wound up, take some slow, steady breaths. And, if there's no one around, roll your shoulders and shake out it out!

TRAIL BLAZIN'

Who wants to look like a clone? It's cooler to blaze your own trail! Wear the colours you love, pick some unique accessories and rock your look, your way!

THE STARDOLL COOL-O-METER

Kawaii

FOLLOW YOUR HEART

The world would be a big ball of boring if no one believed in themselves! Follow your heart, it's the coolest thing you can do!

Going up!

Being yourself, no matter what

Following your dreams

Rocking your own look

Dressing the same as everyone else

Keeping your talents hidden

Going down!

The school of cool!

THE COOL COLLECTION

Design your own collection of clothes with 'cool' as your theme. Log onto Stardoll and head to the Fashion Design studio. Create cool fabric patterns by dragging the shape templates onto the canvas. When you've designed your pattern, click 'choose' to save your fabric. Pick the garment you want to make, drag the sewing pattern onto your fabric and click 'sew'. What will you design?

YOU'RE A PRO

The coolest people are the ones who are totally happy with who they are. Ok, it would be kinda fun to have Emma Watson's wardrobe, but look at the big picture, honey! When it comes to being you, you're a true professional.

WHO CARES WHAT'S HOT AND WHAT'S NOT? IT'S UP TO YOU TO DECIDE WHAT YOU THINK IS COOL.

How to avoid being typecast

BE EVERYTHING!

If there's something you just know you'd be good at, don't keep it to yourself! Get out there and do your thing! Try out a totally new hobby, revamp your style or chat to someone new. Keep trying new things and you'll never, ever be typecast. And that's a fact!

STARDOLL DICTIONARY

Typecast: *1. To cast an actor in a part that's similar to other roles they've played. 2. To expect somebody to do the same thing every day and never try anything different.*

YAWN!

SWITCH UP YOUR STYLE

Being known for your signature style is kind of cool, but what happens when you want to try something new? Fear not, fashionistas! When it comes to your look, you make the rules! Head to the Starbazaar and dress your MeDoll in a totally new way. If you're usually into the casual look, try dressing her for the red carpet. And if you normally go for glam, why not pick an outfit that's totally rock? It's all up to you!

THINK DIFFERENTLY!

MIX UP YOUR WARDROBE

You don't have to go on a massive shopping spree every time you want to change your style. Mix things up by wearing your clothes in a whole new way! Ever tried wearing a top over one of your dresses? How about teaming a shirt with a belt? There are heaps of different ways you can give your clothes a fresh new look.

A GIRL CAN CHANGE HER STYLE WHENEVER SHE LIKES!

UNLEASH A NEW TALENT!

Ever wondered if you'd be awesome at surfing or brilliant at writing? Or maybe you could tame puppies with your fabulous animal skills? Try as many new things as you can to discover your hidden talents!

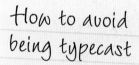

How to avoid being typecast

☑ Think differently

☑ Try new styles

☑ Talk to somebody new

☑ Discover hidden talents

☑ Be your awesome self

Don't stress it!

RELAXATION STATION

Let's face it, even pop stars don't have stress-free lives. And when things are getting too much, a girl needs time to relax. Doing something that makes you feel calm, like drawing or reading, is a great way to kick back.

TALK IT OUT

When stress and worry come your way, talk things through with the people you trust. Getting it all out there in the open can help you work out what to do next.

OVERLOAD ALERT!

When you've got a million things going on at once, life can be pretty hectic! If that's you right now, you're in serious need of some Me Time, honey! Take time out, head to your room and chillax! Listen to music, take your MeDoll to the Starbazzar or sketch a new outfit for yourself. Do something you enjoy and feel your stress melt away!

Handling stress and worry can be tough, but if you focus on the things you can change, you could cut your stress down to size! Flip over the page to find out how . . .

Don't stress it!

1 Grab a notebook and draw a line down the middle of the page, to make two columns. Write 'Change' at the top of the first column and 'Can't change' in the second.

Change	Can't change

2 Think about the stuff you are stressed about and sort it into two lists. Say you were worried about performing in a talent contest. That would go in the 'Change' column, because if you practise hard, you'll be brilliant!

3 Ok, now imagine that you're worried about something you can't change, like a test you've already taken or a person who's not well. Even though you really care, there's nothing you can do, so you'd put those things in the 'Can't change' column.

4 When you've finished, read the worries in your 'Can't change' list. You can't fix these ones, so let them flutter down and rest in your mind. Letting go doesn't mean you don't care, you're just showing that you understand the way things are.

5 Now check out the things you can change. You're in charge of these ones, so the next bit's up to you! Talk to people you trust, put together a brilliant plan and start working towards your goals – you can do it!

How to do confidence

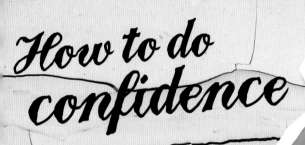

DRUM ROLL, PLEASE!
QUEEN OF CONFIDENCE
COMING THROUGH!

STAND TALL

Girls who walk with their heads
high and their backs straight
ooze confidence and style.
So push your shoulders down
and back, tilt your chin up and
stride out in style. You've got
it, girl!

SPEAK OUT

Picture yourself in a situation where you'd like to express your opinion. Practise what you'd like to say in your mind, then speak the words out loud. Try out different ways of saying the same thing, so you're fully prepared to have your say. Nice work!

POSITIVE THINKING

In the morning, before you leave the house, picture yourself sailing confidently through the day, saying the right things and impressing the world with your all-round awesomeness. Think positive thoughts about yourself and feel that confidence glow around you.

MAGICAL POWERS

Do you believe in the magic of fashion? Of course you do! Clothes can totally transform the way you feel and you know it! Get together with your BF and put together some outfits that will fill you with confidence.

How to do confidence

BEAT THE BLUSH!

Keep your cheeks under control with this clever technique . . .

When you're embarrassed, your body releases a hormone called adrenaline. Adrenaline speeds up your breathing and heart rate, and causes your blood vessels to expand – which means more blood flows around your body and up to your cheeks. If you want to beat the blush, you need to stop that adrenaline in its tracks! You can do that by staying calm and relaxed.

In the privacy of your own room, practise taking deep breaths. Let your breath out slowly and say the word 'calm' slowly in your mind. Take ten nice, relaxing breaths and notice how different you feel. Do this every day, to teach your body how to feel calm.

CHEEKS OF ICE!

Ok, so when you next find yourself in a totally blush-worthy situation, say the word 'calm' in your mind, just like you did back at home. Slow your breathing down and imagine a cool breeze blowing against your face. So long, blush babe! Hello, confidence queen!

Sweet dreams!

Follow these tips for the perfect night's sleep . . .

HELLO, SUNSHINE!

Weirdly enough, a good night's sleep starts in the morning! If you set your alarm for the same time each day, it's easier for your body clock to stay in sync. That means, when it's time to go to bed, your body knows it should relax and rest.

PSSSST!

Lying in at the weekends can mess with your body clock and make it harder for you to sleep at night. Eeek!

SWITCH OFF!

The light from TVs and computers will make your brain want to stay alert and awake. If you switch them off at least half an hour before bed, you'll give your brain a chance to wind down.

RIGHT ON TIME

When you're right in the middle of doing something, the last thing you want to do is stop and go to bed! Get the timing right, so you can finish what you're doing before it's time to hit the sack.

BUBBLE, BUBBLE!

Ok, so scientists haven't proved that bubbles actually help you sleep, but taking a warm bath definitely helps you to relax! You could even add a few drops of lavender essential oil and turn your bath into an aromatherapy treatment.

DEAR DIARY . . .

Writing a diary is a great way to relax before bed. Oh, and if you suddenly remember something you have to do tomorrow, jot that down, too.

THE COMFORT ZONE

Turn your bed into a sanctuary of comfort and calm! Put on your most comfortable PJs, grab all the books and magazines you need, then kick back and relax. Reading is the perfect way to chill before you switch off the light.

YOU ARE GOING TOOOOO SLEEEEEEP!

Hypnotists often ask their patients to count backwards, because it helps their minds to relax. If you're having trouble switching off, try counting down from 200. Don't worry if you lose track, just keep saying numbers in your head. By the time your reach zero, you should be totally chilled.

How to be totally original

"I'm going to do what I want to do. I'm going to be who I really am."

Emma Watson

YOUR ORIGINAL STORY!

Imagine you're sitting in the cinema right now, watching the story of your life on screen. What do you want to happen next? What kind of girl do you want to be? You're the star in your own life story, so it's up to you to decide . . .

"I know what I like, I know what I want, and I know who I want to be."

Jessie J

TOTALLY YOU

Show the world you're unique by wearing clothes and accessories that really say something about you! If you want to make your look even more individual, why not personalise some clothes and accessories? Cover the sleeves of a t-shirt in sequins, or make your own charm bracelet – just do your own thing!

"I love what I wear, I mean I love choosing what I wear."

Kristen Stewart

FOLLOW YOUR DESTINY

When it comes to being yourself, you're officially an expert. So what if you don't fit in every now and then? It's better to stand out from the crowd than be herded along like a sheep. You were born a true original, so don't change a thing. Be yourself every day – that's your destiny!

"Being cool is being your own self, not doing something that someone else is telling you to do."

Vanessa Hudgens

BREAK AWAY

Whether we're talking fashion, adventure or friends, if you want to try something new then don't let anyone hold you back. Some opportunities only come along once, so don't miss your chance! Be your own true self and break away from the crowd!

Make your dreams come true

You know when you watch a TV programme and they show everyone getting ready for a competition? And the camera whizzes around showing the characters doing a teeny bit of practise. Then BAM! Suddenly it's competition day and they've magically won the big prize! If only, right? Everybody knows it's not that easy! If you want to make things happen for real, you've got to practise like crazy and keep working towards your goals. That's what really gets you closer to your dreams . . .

BE THE BEST!

If you believe in yourself, you can do things that you never even dreamed were possible! So stand tall and be as awesome as you know you can be!

SUPERSIZE YOUR DREAMS!

Who says you can only have one dream? Why can't you be a brilliant horse rider and a brilliant fashion designer? Who says you can't dance like a pro and style your way onto Cover Girl? When it comes to dreams, it's up to you to decide what you want to achieve – so dare to dream big, honey!

Make your dreams come true

STAY STRONG

If you want to get really good at something, you've got to stay strong! Look for ways you can improve your skills. Search out all the best opportunities and never give up!

"You've got to work really hard at it. Just don't give up."

Taylor Swift

TOTALLY DREAMY

Meeting other people who share your dreams can be totally inspirational! Hey, why not set up your own club on Stardoll? Then you can meet up with other Stardolls to swap tips and get inspired!

Star sign style

Aries
MARCH 21ST – APRIL 19TH

You're not afraid to stand out from the crowd.
Style it up in tailored trousers.
Style it down in printed playsuits.
Star-matched mates: Taurus, Sagittarius, Aquarius

Taurus
APRIL 20TH – MAY 19TH

You've got a talent for solving problems.
Style it up in cute prom dresses.
Style it down in printed hareem pants.
Star-matched mates: Aries, Scorpio, Capricorn

Gemini
MAY 20TH – JUNE 20TH

You're full of creativity and brilliant ideas.
Style it up in blazers and jackets.
Style it down in pretty maxi skirts.
Star-matched mates: Taurus, Cancer, Sagittarius

Cancer
JUNE 21ST – JULY 22ND

You're always thinking of your friends.
Style it up in retro-print dresses.
Style it down in distressed denims.
Star-matched mates: Gemini, Leo, Pisces

Leo
JULY 23RD – AUGUST 21ST

You're great at boosting people's confidence.
Style it up in tailored shirts.
Style it down in funky leggings.
Star-matched mates: Virgo, Sagittarius, Aquarius

Virgo
AUGUST 22ND – SEPTEMBER 22ND

You're upfront and honest with your friends.
Style it up in lacy dresses.
Style it down in slogan t-shirts.
Star-matched mates: Taurus, Leo, Libra

Libra

SEPTEMBER 23RD – OCTOBER 22ND

You're a brilliant decision maker.
Style it up in halter-neck tops.
Style it down in printed minis.
Star-matched mates: Leo, Virgo, Scorpio

Scorpio

OCTOBER 23RD – NOVEMBER 21ST

You're trustworthy and loyal.
Style it up in smart pencil skirts.
Style it down in kimono tops.
Star-matched mates: Taurus, Virgo, Scorpio

Sagittarius

NOVEMBER 22ND – DECEMBER 21ST

You're adventurous and energetic.
Style it up in glamorous jumpsuits.
Style it down in denim cut-offs.
Star-matched mates: Aries, Gemini, Capricorn

Capricorn

DECEMBER 22ND – JANUARY 20TH

You're determined to follow your dreams.
Style it up in sequined dresses.
Style it down in printed t-shirts.
Star-matched mates: Cancer, Sagittarius,
Aquarius

Aquarius

JANUARY 21ST – FEBRUARY 19TH

You're full of inspirational ideas.
Style it up in boxy jackets.
Style it down in lounge trousers.
Star-matched mates: Aries, Gemini, Pisces

Pisces

FEBRUARY 20TH – MARCH 20TH

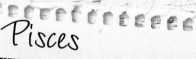

You're in tune with your arty side.
Style it up in high-waisted skirts.
Style it down in crocheted waistcoats.
Star-matched mates: Taurus, Virgo, Aquarius

What's your hidden talent?

What is it about you that makes you so unique?
Follow the arrows to find out!

START

Do you prefer hanging with a few friends or in a big group?

A few friends

Big group

I like to think things over.

False

True

Does your family say you're a chatterbox?

Yes

No

I make decisions quickly.

True

False

I love writing lists and plans.

Nope

Yes

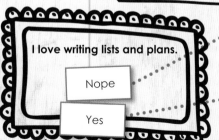
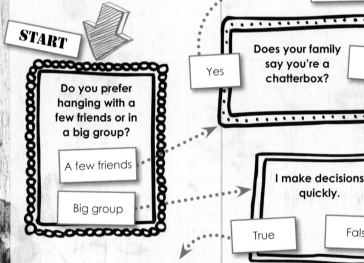

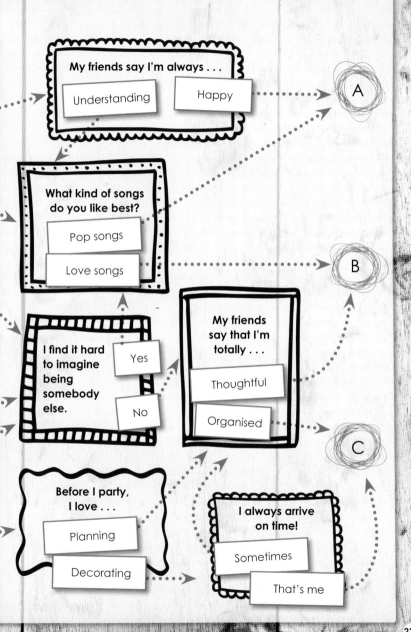

My friends say I'm always . . .

Understanding   Happy

What kind of songs do you like best?

Pop songs

Love songs

I find it hard to imagine being somebody else.

Yes

No

My friends say that I'm totally . . .

Thoughtful

Organised

Before I party, I love . . .

Planning

Decorating

I always arrive on time!

Sometimes

That's me

A

B

C

The Verdict

A Positive Thinker

Your brilliant way of looking at things makes you a handy girl to have around! You've got a talent for seeing the best in everything and you're great at dealing with tricky decisions. Nice work!

B Awesome Instinct

The way you think is really special. You can tune into other people's moods and understand how they're feeling. Your awesome instinct means you make a great BF and a brilliant leader! Go, girl!

C Completely Capable

Whether we're talking party planning or school stuff, you're great at dealing with whatever comes your way. You're independent, organised and capable. No wonder your BFs think you're fab!

The Stardoll guide to being famous . . .

How to get famous!

The road to Starsville starts with talent, so focus on yours right now. We're not just talking singing and acting. Maybe you're an awesome fashion designer, writer or sportsperson? Maybe you've got a skill that's so unique they haven't invented a name for it yet! Focus on whatever it is that YOU do best . . . it's time to follow your dreams!

"I think everything happens for a reason, so there is no such thing as fail."

Mary-Kate Olsen

THINK LIKE A PRO!

Stars-to-be don't wait around hoping for their big break. They think pro and look for ways they can use their talent every day!

"You have to be unique, and different, and shine in your own way."

Lady Gaga

"Give it 110% and don't give up!"

Vanessa Hudgens

KEEP IT REAL!

Who wants to get famous for a crazy publicity stunt? True stars rely on their skill and determination to get them to the top. And that's a fact!

If you're on the bus to Starsville, get ready for a bumpy ride! Nearly every single TV star, singer and author was rejected before they made it big. Even some of the fashion designers you're crazy about were told that they wouldn't make it. The fact is that things don't always work out at first. But so what? You can handle it. Rejection is all part of the journey, right? If you keep working towards your dream, you'll make it through.

"Don't let anyone, or any rejection, keep you from what you want."

Ashley Tisdale

NOW! NOW! NOW!

Could you put together a band or have your own art exhibition? Could you get involved in a school production or a sports club? Take your first steps towards your kind of stardom today!

STYLE IT!

Having rails and rails of gorgeous clothes is all part of being a celeb! But why wait until you're famous? Turn your MeDoll into your celebrity style icon now! Put together a collection of star-worthy outfits, style up for a photoshoot and pose for your Cover Girl shot. Style it out like the star you are!

It's all about the fans!

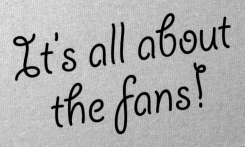

YOU NEVER FORGET YOUR FIRST FANS — THE PEOPLE WHO BELIEVED IN YOU RIGHT FROM THE START.

Here's the thing: you don't have to wait until you're famous to recognise your fans. Look around! You've got a totally awesome fan base already. Think of the friends, family and teachers who all want you to succeed. Those guys are your number one fans, girl! Keep 'em close, and they'll be with you all the way.

TOTALLY INSPIRED!

True stars don't just respect their fans, they look to them for inspiration. When Lady Gaga is on stage she's just as impressed by her fans' outfits as they are by hers! "They get all dressed up," she says. "It's so amazing."

"I think I have the best fans the world . . . As long as I can make them enjoy life a little bit more, I've done my job!"

Zendaya Coleman

Wherever you are in your fame journey, you've got to be true to yourself and true to your fans because let's face it, having a group of fans is a big responsibility. There are people in your life right now who respect your opinions and creativity, so stand up for what you believe in and start being a star role model now. You've got what it takes!

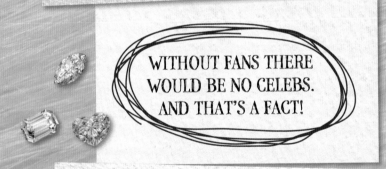

WITHOUT FANS THERE WOULD BE NO CELEBS. AND THAT'S A FACT!

LISTEN UP

True celebs listen to their fans. Think like a star and ask your friends, family and teachers how you can improve your talent. Listen up and use their feedback to take your skill to the next level.

AUTOGRAPH, PLEASE!

Fans LOVE autographs, so make sure yours is a good one! Grab a stack of pens and practise different ways of writing your name. Could you add a stylish swirl? Could you dot your i with a star? Get creative and add a unique touch that's all your own!

Photo frenzy

IF YOU'RE 100% HAPPY
WITH WHAT YOU'RE
WEARING, YOU'LL ALWAYS
BE CAMERA READY!

Whether you're a world famous celeb or a
star-in-training, having your photo taken is
all part of the gig and the first thing celebs-
to-be learn is camera control. You may not
be in charge of taking the pictures, but you
are in control of what you wear and how
you pose. So when those cameras start
snapping, show off your outfit and flash that
Hollywood smile!

MIRROR, MIRROR!

It doesn't matter if it's your snap-happy sister or a truck-load of paparazzi, a girl's got to be prepared for camera action at any time of the day! Get in some serious mirror time and practise the poses that work for you.

ALBUM ACTION!

Want to get ready for a life in the spotlight? Create an awesome album for your MeDoll! Fill your album with fab fashion pictures and get other Stardolls to rate your look. Log on to www.stardoll.com to find out how!

Rock the red carpet!

There are so many opportunities to dress up, why wait 'til you're famous? When you're a celeb-in-training, the whole world is your red carpet and don't you forget it! Whether it's your BF's birthday bash or the opening of the latest blockbuster hit, plan an outfit that will dazzle the crowds!

RED CARPET STYLE!

Your red carpet outfit is big personality statement. Pick a design that truly expresses your inner-celeb!

FOR REAL!

Your first time on the red carpet can be pretty crazy! With all those camera flashing, you'll hardly know where to look first. The secret is to slow down – if you rush past all the photographers, journalists and fans then you won't have any fun! Take some deep breaths, chill out and own that carpet, Stardoll!

SHOW STOPPER!

What would your MeDoll wear to the most exciting event in showbiz history? Design the ultimate red carpet dress for her!

MEDIA SAVVY!

If you're destined for a life in the spotlight, you need to get media savvy! Start by checking out as many TV and magazine interviews as you can. What kind of questions do people ask celebrities? What kind of replies do they give? Think about things from a professional angle and pick up some useful ideas.

HOW TO HANDLE TRICKY QUESTIONS . . .

Want to steer your way through the media maze? This question and answer session will set you on the right track!

"What's the most embarrassing thing that's ever happened to you?"

Eeek! If you answer this with the truth, your worst cringe will be broadcast around the world! Think smart and come up with a less blush-worthy story to give to the press!

"Have you ever regretted any of your style choices?"

Answer this with a detailed description and someone is bound to track down photographic evidence! If that's not ok with you, just say something vague and mysterious!

"Who are your favourite fashion designers?"

Don't just reel off names, here! Add some details about what makes each designer special. Oh, and if you've got your own fashion label, make sure you mention it!

DIVA ALERT!

Have you ever noticed
how true stars never
boast about their
achievements? Listen
to celeb interviews and
you'll hear them say
things like, 'We had
so much fun making
that movie!' and 'I was
so excited to win the
award!' Acknowledging
that you're totally
awesome without
actually showing off is a
tricky skill to master, so
start practising now and
you'll be way ahead of
the game!

OMG! You can't say that . . .

- ☒ "I was the best actor, so I deserved it!"
- ☒ "It was all down to my immense talent!"
- ☒ "What can I say? Everyone loves me!"

Ok, that's better . . .

- ☑ "I was so lucky to get the lead role."
- ☑ "We worked really well as a team!"
- ☑ "I was totally blown away by the fans!"

Design your own fashion label

Singers and actors love designing fashion collections for their fans. Turn your MeDoll into a superstar and design your own celebrity line! Once you've finished, you can sell your unique designs at the StarBazaar. Log on and get creative, honey!

"I want to design my own clothes range."

Jessie J

DESIGN ONLINE!

Creating your own designs on Stardoll is so much fun. Here's how you do it:

Go to the Fashion Design studio and click on Start. Design your own fabric pattern by dragging the shapes you like onto the canvas. Play around with patterns and colours until you find exactly the right look. Once you're happy, choose the garment you'd like to make and drag the sewing pattern over your fabric. Click on sew and your design is ready to wear!

HEY, HAVE YOU TRIED THE FASHION DESIGN STUDIO?

DESIGNER FABRICS

If you're serious about real-world design, you need to know your fabrics, people!

Wool can come from goats, camels and rabbits, as well as sheep. Use it to make jumpers, coats and jackets.

Tweed is a textured wool fabric woven into different patterns. Use it to make skirts, jackets and coats.

Silk is a delicate fabric made from the silk of moth caterpillars. Use it to make evening wear and wedding dresses.

Cotton is a tough, versatile fabric made from cotton plants. Use it to make dresses, jeans and jumpers.

Jersey is a stretchy fabric made of wool, cotton and man-made fibres. Use it to make leggings, dresses and T-shirts.

Viscose is a man-made material that looks lightweight and floaty. Use it to make dresses, skirts and tops.

Dance like a pro!

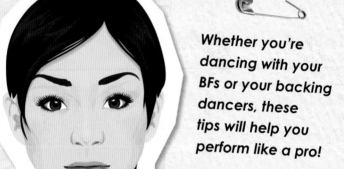

Whether you're dancing with your BFs or your backing dancers, these tips will help you perform like a pro!

WHAT IS IT ABOUT SOME SONGS THAT JUST MAKE YOU WANT TO DANCE?

MUSIC MATTERS

When it comes to chorography, music reeeeaaally matters. If you and your girls love a song, you'll LOVE dancing to it, right? So when you're choosing your music, go with your instincts and pick your top tunes!

STEP ON

If you forget which leg to step on, tap your toe on the ground before you dance! The tap will send a muscle memory to your brain and help you get it right!

ONE, TWO, THREE!

Most songs have regular beats which are spaced out evenly. Beats usually come in groups of two, three or four. Listen to a couple of your favourite tracks and see if you can pick them out. Once you've nailed it, count the beat in your head and build your dance steps around it – that's what choreographers do.

BE CONFIDENT

Dancing on stage can be pretty scary. "I still get nervous in front of a really big crowd," says Bella Thorne. If you're feeling anxious before your performance, just reach out to your BFs. "I always grab Zendaya's hand before I go on stage!" Bella giggles. Her advice is to: "Have confidence in what you're going to do and breathe in and out!"

STARDOLL DICTIONARY

Choreography:

1. The art of planning dances and ballets.

2. Arranging the steps and movements of dancers and where they stand on stage.

COOL CHOREOGRAPHY

When you're teaching a group of people a new routine, you need to get them thinking as one. Switch off the music and count out the beat together. One, two, one, two, one, two. Now walk through the steps as you count out loud. Don't switch the music back on until you're all moving in sync. You'll all soon be dancing in perfect formation!

Wardrobe malfunction!

There is nothing worse than a high-visibility wardrobe malfunction. You know, the kind of fashion disaster that happens in front of a huge crowd? So what should you do if it happens to you? Well, there are two main approaches favoured by the stars. The first is to readjust and act as if nothing happened. The second is to laugh it off and move on. All disasters are different, so go with your instincts . . .

MOVE ON

Whether it's your BFs, your family or the media, if people keep going on about what happened, you don't have to put up with it! Just say 'Yeah, it happened, now let's move on.' They'll soon get the message!

MIRROR IMAGE

Celebs often love the same designs and every now and then, two stars show up in the exact same outfit. If this happens to you, act quickly! Is there something you can borrow to style up your outfit and make it look different? If the answer's no, take a breath, go over to your style twin and tell her you love her look! If you crack a joke, it stops the situation from getting embarrassing!

PSSSST!
AVOID DOING THE MATCHY-MATCHY THING BY MAKING YOUR CLOTHES UNIQUE! STYLE UP OUT-FITS FOR YOU AND YOUR MEDOLL AND WORK YOUR OWN LOOK!

Form your own entourage!

Who needs the experts? You and your BFs make a pretty awesome entourage already! You've all got different talents and you know each other inside-out. It's the perfect arrangement! Get together and decide who'd be best for each job . . .

PICK A VOICE COACH

This is a great role for somebody who can play an instrument or sing. It's up to the voice coach to train your group to sing loud and proud!

PICK A CHOREOGRAPHER

This role is perfect for somebody who's great at explaining tricky dance moves. A choreographer needs to be a teacher as well as a dance star.

PICK A PERSONAL TRAINER

The person who takes on this role needs to be friendly and encouraging, and totally sporty, too. Who's up for the challenge?

PICK A STYLIST

It's going to be way too hard to choose just one person for this job! Be each other's stylists and pick out your celeb-style outfits together.

NOW GET TO WORK COACHING AND SUPPORTING EACH OTHER ON THE ROAD TO STARDOM!

Sweet Suite style

When you join Stardoll you get your own Suite to decorate and if you upgrade to Superstar, you can even get a penthouse!

DREAM DESIGNS

This is your chance to create the designs of your dreams, so decorate your Suite exactly how you like! If you're crazy about animals you might want to add designs inspired by wildlife. Or if you've always dreamt of living by the sea, you could decorate your Suite like a beach house. Bring it on!

TRUE INSPIRATION

Flick through some magazines and find a picture of a room you love. Now jump on Stardoll and recreate the whole look for your Suite! You can create rooms from your favourite TV shows, too! If you can't find what you need in the shop, make it yourself in the Interior Design Studio!

HOW TO USE THE INTERIOR DESIGN STUDIO

First you need to design your fabric, so hop over to the Interior Design Studio and get creative! Next, choose something from the interior collection. It could be a rug, a mirror, a chair . . . whatever you like! Drag the picture over your fabric, click sew and it's ready to go!

STARDOLL'S INTERIOR DESIGN STUDIO IS SO AWESOME! HAVE YOU TRIED IT YET?

What's your fame factor?

Start here

Do you love dressing in glittery outfits?

Sometimes

Oh, yeah

'I'm always telling jokes to my friends!'

So true

Not really

What's the best plan for tonight?

Dance party

Girls' night

Have you ever been told off for talking in class?

No, never

I admit it

Can you play any musical instruments?

Nope

Yes

Getting use to being famous would take me:

Less than a week

More than a week

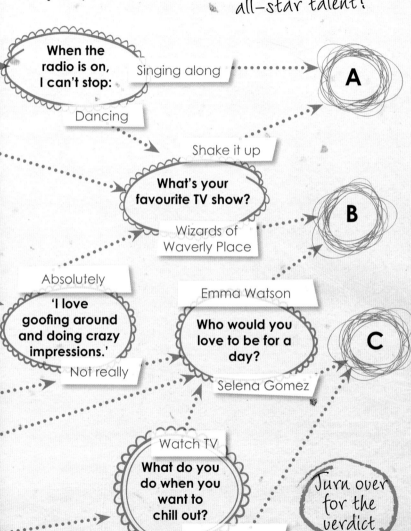

Pssst! What would you be famous for? Follow the arrows to reveal your all-star talent!

When the radio is on, I can't stop:

Singing along → **A**

Dancing

Shake it up

What's your favourite TV show?

B

Wizards of Waverly Place

Absolutely

Emma Watson

'I love goofing around and doing crazy impressions.'

Who would you love to be for a day?

C

Not really

Selena Gomez

Watch TV

What do you do when you want to chill out?

Listen to music

Turn over for the verdict

267

The verdict

A Dance Diva!

MAKE IT HAPPEN

You've got the moves, honey! You're a natural born dancer.
Get together with your BFs and form a dance troupe.
Get noticed by auditioning for performances.

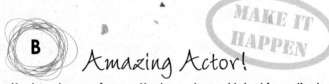

B Amazing Actor!

MAKE IT HAPPEN

You're a true performer. You've got a real talent for acting!
Practise learning lines and reading plays in your room.
Get noticed at a drama group or a school production.

C Singing Star!

MAKE IT HAPPEN

**With your talent and determination, you could
be a singer for sure!**
Develop your voice by singing different songs.
Get noticed by singing in a show choir or musical.

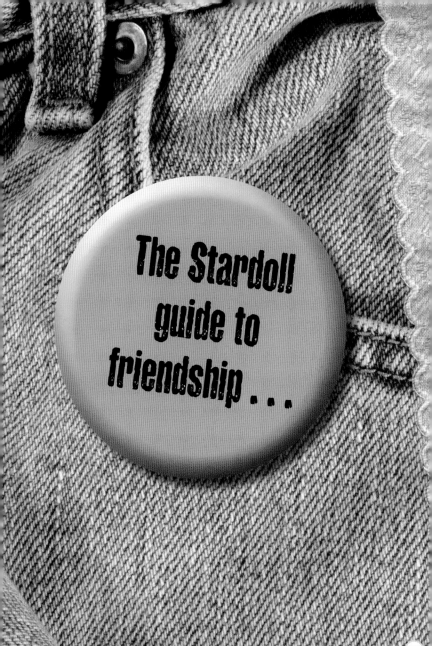

The Stardoll guide to friendship . . .

How to be a fabulous BF

Celebrate your brilliant friendship by being even more fabulous than usual!

PAMPER PARTNERS

Get together with your BF and give each other a face mask or a manicure. Spending time hanging out and being totally fabulous together will make your friendship officially awesome!

KNOW THE SMALL STUFF

Knowing loads of funny little details about your friend will make her feel super-special. Do you know her dream holiday destination? How about the name of her first teddy bear? Get to know the small stuff and your BFF bond will be even stronger.

LET HER TALK

It's official! Good listeners make fabulous friends. If your BF is trying to tell you something, don't rush her along or interrupt what she's saying. Whether she's telling you about something funny or opening up about her feelings, let her do it in her own sweet time.

TOTALLY TRUTHFUL

When friends are truthful with each other, they know they can trust one another, no matter what. Make a deal with your BF that you'll always be honest about the stuff that really counts. That way, you'll both have someone you can rely on. How fabulous is that?

The Stardoll etiquette guide

You can make loads of new friends on Stardoll!
But you should always be careful online, so make
sure you follow these simple rules . . .

DOs

★ Enjoy yourself and have as much
fun as you can!

★ Get creative! Inspire yourself and
be an inspiration to others.

★ Create and dress up the coolest MeDolls
ever! Get styling, honey!

★ Hang out with your BFs and make
heaps of new friends, too.

★ Be fabulous to each other and
respect other people's ideas,
styles and beliefs.

DON'Ts

⭐ Never give out your password, email addresses or any other personal information.

⭐ Never ask other Stardolls for their passwords, email addresses or other personal information.

⭐ Never give out real world photographs of yourself.

⭐ Never use bad language or rude words.

⭐ Never be unkind or mean to other Stardolls.

Want to check out the rules in full? Go to www.stardoll.com and click on 'Rules & Safety' at the bottom of the page. Another page will come up – to read the rules, click on 'Stardoll Etiquette – our One-Stop Rules'.

It's personal!

What is personal information? Well, it's the stuff that is personal to you, and only to you. Let's take a look at what this includes, so that you know for sure!

PERSONAL INFO:

- ☑ Your real name
- ☑ Your birthday
- ☑ Your email address
- ☑ Your home address
- ☑ Your mobile phone number
- ☑ Your home phone number
- ☑ Photos of you, your friends and your family
- ☑ Your passwords

PSSST!
THE NAME OF YOUR SCHOOL AND OTHER PLACES YOU LIKE TO GO TO ARE ALSO PERSONAL. SO KEEP THEM HUSH HUSH ON STARDOLL!

The perfect password

You're bound to have many, many passwords for the important, and sometimes top-secret, things in your life. But just because you have loads of them to remember, doesn't mean you should choose easy to remember passwords! Here are our top tips for picking the perfect password . . .

TOP TIP

Mix things up, by using a combination of both letters and numbers. If it's a case-sensitive password, you could add some capital letters in there, too!

TOP TIP

Change your password every few months, to make it more different for others to keep track of it or suss it out!

TOP TIP

Don't use obvious words or number combos, like your name or your date of birth. These would be other people's first guess!

TOP TIP

Don't write your passwords down anywhere. Who knows who might find them and then use them, Stardolls!

TOP TIP

Use a different password for each thing. If you use the same password every time, then if someone cracks the code then they will have access to ALL your stuff!

Rock your friendship!

There's no-one else quite like your best friend.
Here's how to make her feel special . . .

Lend her your favourite dress to wear to a party.

Tell her the craziest jokes ever and make her laugh until she cries.

Share half of your chocolate bar with her, even if it's your fave!

Let her borrow your pens when she's forgotten her pencil case.

If you take a bad photo of her, delete it before anyone sees!

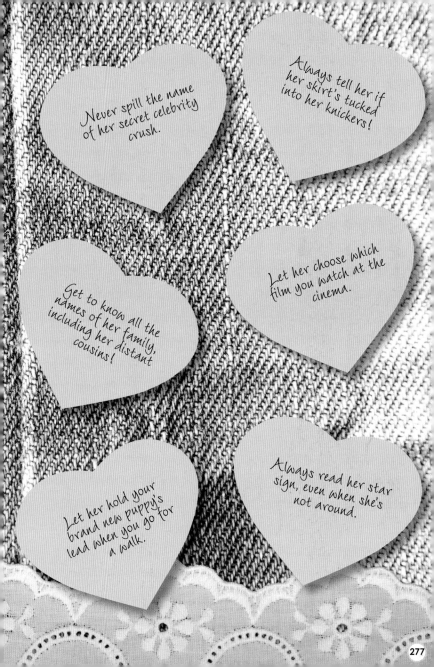

Never spill the name of her secret celebrity crush.

Always tell her if her skirt's tucked into her knickers!

Get to know all the names of her family, including her distant cousins!

Let her choose which film you watch at the cinema.

Let her hold your brand new puppy's lead when you go for a walk.

Always read her star sign, even when she's not around.

Best friend blues

Blast your blues away with these fab friendship tips!

DO YOUR THING

It's kinda cool when you and your BF share some of the same hobbies. But what if your hobbies just don't match up? Hey, it's ok if you're crazy about horses and she's mad about dance! Being into different stuff doesn't mean you're not BFs – in fact, doing separate things can actually make your friendship stronger.

CHANGING TIMES

Best friends need each other when there's something to celebrate and also when things get rough. Share the fun stuff and the tough stuff and you'll always be friends, no matter what!

NEW FRIEND ALERT!

If your BF makes a new friend, don't panic! It doesn't mean you two are over, just because she's hanging with someone new. Include the new girl in a few of your plans, but save some time for just you and your BF, too. That way you'll all be able to hang out and have fun!

KEEP CARING

If your friend is feeling blue, show her that you care! Listen if she just wants to talk, or suggest you get out and do something fun together. With you by her side, she'll soon be feeling better!

Long-distance friendship

If one of you moves away, it doesn't mean that your friendship is doomed! There's still heaps of fun to be had, even when you're far apart . . .

BEST FRIENDS FOREVER

Talk to your parents about how you and your BF can keep in touch. Could you write letters or emails? Could you call or Skype? Make a plan so you know you can keep close, no matter how far apart you actually are.

PARTY TIME

You know what? You two can hang out at Stardoll parties anytime you want! You could even make a pact to go to a party together every week. If you want to plan your MeDolls' outfits before the big event, just hop on email or IM and talk it over!

POSTCARD PING-PONG

You need some sticky labels and a postcard to play this long-distance game. Leaving most of the postcard blank, write a tiny message on the card in your smallest writing. Next, write your BF's address in normal writing and pop the card in the post. When your friend gets the card, she writes a tiny message herself, sticks a label over her address and writes your address on top. See how many times you can ping-pong the same postcard back and forth!

Friendship fall-outs

Fights and fall-outs officially suck, but don't despair! There are heaps of ways to fix your problems. You just need to think smart and work your way through it . . .

THINK IT THROUGH . . .

TAKE SOME TIME TO COOL DOWN. IT'S HARD TO MAKE UP WHEN YOU'RE STILL FEELING ANGRY.

CAN YOU THINK OF A CALMER WAY TO EXPLAIN HOW YOU FEEL? NO SHOUTING ALLOWED, STARDOLLS!

ARE YOU WILLING TO LISTEN TO YOUR FRIEND WITHOUT INTERRUPTING HER? IT'S ONLY FAIR!

FRIENDSHIP FIRST

If you're ready to talk, kick things off by focusing on your friendship rather than the fight. Let your BF know how important she is and how much you love hanging out. Tell her you want to work things out and ask if she's ready to talk . . .

GROUP FALL-OUTS

It's kind of hard to talk things through if there's a whole group of you! If everyone starts talking at once, you'll never sort things out! Before you talk, make a deal to listen to each other without interrupting, then you'll all get a chance to be heard.

STUCK IN THE MIDDLE

Sometimes fall-outs can affect you, even if you're not the one who is fighting! If your friends have fallen out with each other it can seem like you're stuck in the middle. If that's you right now, explain how you're feeling to your mates. Help them work things out if you can, but don't forget that it's not up to you to fix their fight – only they can do that, right?

GET HAPPY!

Spending time away from your BF can be hard, but taking time out to do your own thing is often all it takes to mend a broken friendship. Think about some fun ways to spend your time and just follow your heart! If you get out there and do your thing, you'll soon be feeling heaps happier about everything!

How to handle a copycat

Life can get tricky when a friend keeps copying your look, but before you tell her to cut it out, take time to think things through. Could there be a reason why she keeps stealing your style? Is she feeling insecure about her own fashion sense? Girls who behave like copycats often just don't feel confident in themselves. And if your friend's feeling like that, she's going to need your support, right?

COMPLIMENTS, COMPLIMENTS!

Instead of pointing out that you're both wearing the same top, mention something individual about her outfit, like her necklace or her shoes. Complimenting her style choices will help to boost her confidence.

HIT THE SHOPS

Go on a shopping trip together and help your mate pick an outfit that's totally unique!

STARDOLL TO THE RESCUE!

Have a Stardoll styling session and encourage her to try out some new looks. Making her MeDoll look awesome will encourage your friend to have fun with fashion!

PSSSST!

If other people like your clothes so much they want to copy them, that officially makes you a trendsetter! Which means you're following in the footsteps of famous designers like Mary Quant, Coco Chanel and Vivienne Westwood. Sweet!

FRIENDSHIP TRIANGLES

When you've got two best friends, you never get bored! You could form your own band, throw a fashion show, plan a Stardoll party and do heaps and heaps of other cool stuff . . .

CLUB TOGETHER

Having a group of three is kind of like being in a club, so why not make things official? Come up with a cool club name and plan loads of awesome activities and events!

TALK IT OVER

Make a group promise to talk about your feelings, so you can sort out any friendship tangles straight away.

POWER PLANNING

You don't have to do everything in a group, right? But if you're making arrangements with just one of your BFs, make sure your other buddy doesn't feel left out. If you're making plans in a pair, plan something as a group at the same time, so everyone's included!

TALENT TRIO!

Having two BFs can help you take your talent to the next level, because when you need practical advice and honest opinions, you'll have two experts right there to help you out! Awesome!

Friendship fortune cookies

Make these delicious friendship fortune cookies, with a secret message in each one!

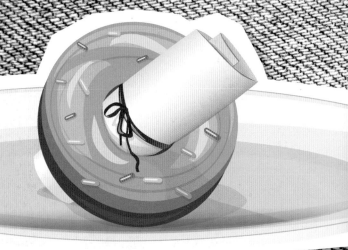

YOU'LL NEED:

Ingredients

100g butter
225g plain flour
½ teaspoon baking powder
40g sugar
2 egg yolks
Tube of ready-made pink icing
Sugar sprinkles

Cooking equipment

Mixing bowl
Baking tray
Sieve
Wooden spoon
Rolling pin
Cookie cutters
Apple corer
Wire rack

Friendship fortunes

Pink card
Pencil
Safety scissors

ASK AN ADULT TO HELP YOU!

BEFORE YOU START

Pre-heat the oven to 180°C/375°F/ gas mark 4.

1 Grease the baking tray with a little bit of butter. Cut the rest of the butter into small cubes and set it aside. Sift the flour and baking powder into a bowl and add the cubes of butter.

2 Put your hands in the bowl and rub the butter and flour together with your fingertips, until the mixture looks like breadcrumbs. Stir in the sugar.

3 Add your egg yolks and stir them into the mixture with a spoon until everything binds together to form a stiff dough. Now use your hands to make the dough into a ball.

4 Dust your rolling pin and work surface with flour. Roll out the dough until it's about 5mm thick. Cut out your cookies with your cookie cutter and use the apple corer to make a hole in the middle of each cookie.

5 Place your cookies on the baking tray. Bake them for 10-12 minutes until they're golden. Carefully take them out the oven and leave them to cool for five minutes, then put them on the wire rack. Decorate your cookies with icing and sprinkles.

6 While the icing is drying, use a pair of scissors to cut your pink card into 5cm x 3cm strips. Write a different friendship fortune on each strip of card. Now roll your friendship fortunes into scrolls and slot them through the holes in your cookies.

FRIENDSHIP FORTUNES

Copy these fortunes onto your pink card, or make up some of your own!

WE'LL BE FRIENDS FOREVER AND EVER!

COME TO MY HOUSE FOR MOVIES AND POPCORN.

PSSST! I'LL ALWAYS KEEP YOUR SECRETS.

COME TO MY STARDOLL PARTY!

YOU CAN BORROW MY FAVOURITE DRESS.

What's your friendship force?

What kind of BF are you? Just follow the arrows to find out!

Start here

What do you love most about sleepovers with your BF?
- Dance routines
- Girly chats

What do you like most about your BFs birthday?
- Giving presents
- Having a party

What are you most likely to borrow from your BF?
- Her accessories
- Her clothes

Do you and your BF have the same taste in music?
- All the time
- Sometimes

How would you cheer up a miserable mate?
- Give her a hug
- Tell her a joke

What do you do most when you're together?
- Talk
- Laugh

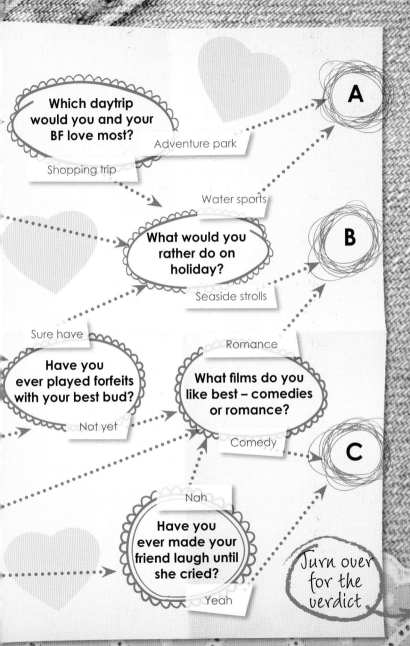

FRIENDSHIP FORCE FACTOR

A *Whirlwind of Adventure*

Woo hoo! With an adventurous friend like you, there's never a dull moment for your best bud – you're a total whirlwind!

FRIENDSHIP FORCE FACTOR

B *Gentle Breeze*

Your BF is very lucky to have a friend like you. You're so thoughtful and easy going – life's a breeze when you're around!

FRIENDSHIP FORCE FACTOR

C Hurricane

Wow, honey! You're a blast! When you and your BF get together, you both laugh harder than a hurricane – bring on the giggles!

Hi again, Stardolls! It's me, Ami!

Hey, it's official! Now you've reached the end
of the Style Bible, you're more stylish than ever before!
In fact, you've probably blasted right off the end
of the Stardoll style-o-meter. When it comes to being
original and unique, you've got it nailed!

Why not put all your awesome new knowledge to the
test? Head over to stardoll.com and try out your
favourite style tribes! You could even style up your
MeDoll in her Stardoll colours — just hop back to
page 74 to find out if she's fresh, fierce or fabulous!

Oooh, maybe you could get your friends over for
a natural home spa or a party soon? I can't wait to
play the icebreakers on page 168! Let's face it, people.

When you know how to live your life in style, there's always something exciting to do!

I've got to sign off for now, but will you come over and say hi? My account name is Ami.Stardoll

Stay fabulous and keep following your dreams!

Lots of love

Ami x

MAKE YOUR OWN UNIQUE OUTFITS IN THE STARDESIGN STUDIO. CHOOSE YOUR COLOURS, CREATE YOUR FABRIC PATTERN, THEN DESIGN AN AWESOME OUTFIT FOR YOUR MEDOLL!

THROW A PARTY AND INVITE ALL YOUR FRIENDS TO COME ALONG FOR A CHAT! CHOOSE A PARTY ROOM, DECORATE IT AND THEN GET YOUR PARTY STARTED!

We ♥ Stardoll!

CREATE GORGEOUS THINGS FOR YOUR SUITE IN STARDOLL'S INTERIOR DESIGN STUDIO. DESIGN YOUR OWN SOFAS, RUGS, TABLES, PHOTO FRAMES . . . YOU CAN MAKE WHATEVER YOU LIKE!

JOIN COOL CLUBS AND SHARE YOUR HOBBIES WITH OTHER STARDOLLS. THERE ARE FASHION CLUBS, PET CLUBS, MUSIC CLUBS . . . TAKE YOUR PICK, HONEY!

GO SHOPPING AT THE STARPLAZA, AND IF YOUR MEDOLL HAS SUPERSTAR STATUS, YOU CAN SHOP FOR EXCLUSIVE DESIGNS AT THE STARBAZAAR! JUST DRESS HOW YOU FEEL!